CONTEMPORARY PLAYWRIGHTS

TOM STOPPARD
BY
RONALD HAYMAN

SECOND EDITION

HEINEMANN · LONDON

Heinemann Educational Books Ltd
London   Edinburgh   Melbourne   Auckland   Toronto
Hong Kong   Singapore   Kuala Lumpur
Ibadan   Nairobi   Johannesburg
Lusaka   New Delhi
Kingston

ISBN (U.K) 0 435 18441 5 (paper)
ISBN (U.K.) 0 435 18440 7 (cased)

Published by Heinemann Educational Books Ltd
48 Charles Street, London W1X 8AH
Printed Offset Litho and bound in Great Britain by
Cox & Wyman Ltd, London, Fakenham and Reading

CONTENTS

ACKNOWLEDGEMENTS

I am extremely grateful to Tom Stoppard not only for the two interviews which begin and end the book but for co-operating on editing the transcripts of them, and for reading through the whole text and correcting some errors. The first interview originally appeared—with some critical comment spatchcocked into it—as a 'Profile of Tom Stoppard' in the December 1974 issue of *The New Review* and I am most grateful to the Editor, Ian Hamilton, for commissioning the piece and starting me on the process of the thinking which has culminated in this book. I must also acknowledge a valuable incentive towards writing it: Clive James's generosity about the Profile in his *Encounter* article on Stoppard (November 1975).

The photograph of *Rosencrantz and Guildenstern Are Dead* is reproduced by courtesy of the National Theatre, photo by Anthony Crickmay; that of *After Magritte* by courtesy of Inter-Action Trust; that of *Jumpers* by courtesy of the National Theatre, photo by Zoë Dominic; and that of *Travesties* by courtesy of the Governors of the Royal Shakespeare Theatre, Stratford-upon-Avon.

The cover photograph of Tom Stoppard is reproduced by permission of Philip Gaskell.

NOTE ON SECOND EDITION

I have added a chapter on *Every Good Boy Deserves Favour*, the play for actors and symphony orchestra, and on *Professional Foul*, the television play. I have also updated the reference sections.

BIOGRAPHICAL OUTLINE

1937   Born 3 July in Czechoslovakia, the son of Eugene Straussler, a doctor employed by Bata, the shoe manufacturers.

1939   The family moved to Singapore.

1942   Evacuated to India with his mother and brother before the Japanese invasion. His father, who remained behind, was killed. His mother became manageress of a Bata shoe shop in Darjeeling. He went to a multi-racial English-speaking school in Darjeeling.

1946   She married Kenneth Stoppard, who was in the British army in India. The family left for England, where he worked in the machine tool business.

1946-54   Educated at a prep school in Nottinghamshire, and a grammar school in Yorkshire.

ca 1950   The family settled in Bristol.

1954-60   Employed by the Western Daily Press in Bristol and (from 1958) by the Bristol Evening World as news reporter, feature writer, theatre critic, film critic and gossip columnist.

1960   Finished *A Walk on the Water*—later called *Enter a Free Man*.

1960-62   Freelance journalism. Work included critical articles and two pseudonymous weekly columns.

1963   Drama critic for *Scene*. Within seven months he saw 132 plays. Wrote short stories, three of which were bought by Faber. Commissioned by the publisher Anthony Blond to write a novel.

1964   May to October visit to Berlin on a Ford Foundation Grant. Commissioned to write two short plays for Radio 4 and five episodes of the serial *The Dales* for Radio 4. Wrote *Rosencrantz and Guildenstern Meet King Lear*, a one-act play in verse.

1965   Married Jose Ingle. The Royal Shakespeare Company

bought an option on *Rosencrantz and Guildenstern Are Dead*. Wrote regular weekly episodes of *A Student's Diary* (An Arab in London) transmitted in Arabic by the BBC.

1967   Won the John Whiting award and an *Evening Standard* award.

1968   Won the Prix Italia for *Albert's Bridge*.

1972   Married Dr Miriam Moore-Robinson, who later became medical director of a pharmaceutical company and later deputy managing director. Made *Tom Stoppard Doesn't Know* for the BBC television series *One Pair of Eyes*.

1973   Directed Garson Kanin's *Born Yesterday* at Greenwich.

1974   Contracted to work on the screenplay for Joseph Losey's film of Thomas Wiseman's *The Romantic Englishwoman*.

1976   Edited *Hamlet* into a 15-minute version for Inter-Action.

1977   Visits to Moscow and Leningrad with the assistant director of the British section of Amnesty International and to Prague.

BIBLIOGRAPHY

Texts

Enter a Free Man
Rosencrantz and Guildenstern Are Dead
Albert's Bridge and *If You're Glad I'll Be Frank*
The Real Inspector Hound
After Magritte
Jumpers
Artist Descending a Staircase
Travesties
Dirty Linen and *New-Found-Land*

All these have been published by Faber and Faber, who have
also reprinted Tom Stoppard's novel *Lord Malquist and Mr
Moon*, originally published by Anthony Blond. Inter-Action has
published a limited edition of *Dirty Linen* and *New-Found-
Land*. *A Separate Peace* is published in *Playbill Two*, ed. Alan
Durband (Hutchinson).

Select Bibliography of Articles and Interviews

1967   'The Devious Road to Waterloo' (with Keith Harper),
        The Guardian, 7 April.
        'The Positive Maybe', *Author*, No 78, Spring.
        'Writing's My 43rd Priority' (with John Gale), *The
        Observer*, 17 December.
1968   'Something to Declare', *The Sunday Times*, 25
        February.
        'Tom Stoppard' (with Giles Gordon), *Transatlantic
        Review*, No 29, Summer; (Reprinted in *Behind the
        Scenes*, ed. Joseph F. McCrindle, Pitman)
1971   Commentary on *Orghast* by Ted Hughes, *Times*

Literary Supplement, 1 October.

'Yes We Have No Banana', *The Guardian*, 10 December.

1972 'Tom Stoppard and the Contentment of Insecurity' (with Barry Norman), *The Times*, 11 November.

1973 'Interview with Tom Stoppard' (with Janet Watts), *The Guardian*, 21 March.

'The Translators: Tom Stoppard' (with Michael Leech), *Plays and Players*, April.

'Playwrights and Professors', *Times Literary Supplement*, 13 October.

1974 'Ambushes for the Audience: Towards a High Comedy of Ideas' (with the Editors of *Theatre Quarterly*), *Theatre Quarterly*, Vol IV No 14, May-July.

'The Joke's the Thing' (with Mark Amory), *Observer Magazine*, 9 June.

'Tom Stoppard' (with A.C.H. Smith), *Flourish*, RSC Club News-sheet, 1974, issue 1.

1977 'The Face at the Window', *Sunday Times*, 27 February. An account of his visit to Moscow and Leningrad.

'But for the Middle Classes', *Times Literary Supplement*, 3 June. A preview of Paul Johnson's *Enemies of Society*.

Criticism of Tom Stoppard

1. Books with chapters on Stoppard or extended references
   Robert Brustein, *The Third Theatre*, Cape 1970.
   John Russell Taylor, *Anger and After*, second ed. Methuen 1969; *The Second Wave*, Methuen 1971.
2. Articles in Periodicals and Newspapers
   A.J. Ayer, 'Love among the Logical Positivists', *The Sunday Times*, 9 April 1972.
   Jonathan Bennett, 'Philosophy and Mr Stoppard', *Philosophy* 50, January 1975.
   Anthony Callen, 'Stoppard's Godot: Some French Influences on Postwar English Drama', *New Theatre Magazine*, Winter 1969.

Richard Ellmann, 'The Zealots of Zurich', *Times Literary Supplement*, 12 July 1974.

Clive James, 'Count Zero Splits the Infinite', *Encounter*, November 1975.

3. Pamphlets

C.W.E. Bigsby, *Tom Stoppard* 'Writers and their Work', Longmans for British Council 1976.

Bibliography

Theatre Checklist No 2. 'Tom Stoppard' in *Theatrefacts* No 2, published by *Theatre Quarterly* Publications May-July 1974.

PERFORMANCES

November 1963	*A Walk on the Water* transmitted by ITV, directed by Peter Moffatt (adaptation of the stage play which later became *Enter a Free Man*).
1964	Staged at Hamburg.
February 1964	*The Dissolution of Dominic Boot* broadcast by the BBC, produced by Michael Bakewell.
April 1964	*'M' Is for Moon among Other Things* broadcast by the BBC, produced by John Tydeman.
1965	*The Gamblers* produced by the Drama Department of Bristol University.
February 1966	*If You're Glad I'll Be Frank* broadcast by the BBC, produced by John Tydeman.
August 1966	*Rosencrantz and Guildenstern Are Dead*, on the fringe of the Edinburgh Festival produced by the Oxford Theatre Group directed by Brian Daubney.
August 1966	*A Separate Peace* transmitted by BBC Television, directed by Alan Gibson with John Wood and John Stride.
February 1967	*Teeth* transmitted by BBC Television, directed by Alan Gibson.
April 1967	*Rosencrantz and Guildenstern Are Dead* presented by the National Theatre at the Old Vic, directed by Derek Goldby with John Stride and Edward Petherbridge.
June 1967	*Another Moon Called Earth* transmitted by BBC Television, directed by Alan Gibson.
July 1967	*Albert's Bridge* broadcast by BBC Television, produced by Charles Lefeaux.
March 1968	*Enter a Free Man* at the St Martin's, directed by Frith Banbury with Michael Hordern

and Megs Jenkins.

June 1968	*The Real Inspector Hound* at the Criterion Theatre, directed by Robert Chetwyn with Richard Briers and Ronnie Barker.
December 1968	*Neutral Ground* transmitted by Thames Television, directed by Piers Haggard.
August 1969	*Albert's Bridge* and *If You're Glad I'll Be Frank*, on the fringe of the Edinburgh Festival, directed by Henry Murry.
March 1970	*The Engagement* (a new version of *The Dissolution of Dominic Boot*) transmitted by NBC Television in the United States, directed by Paul Joyce.
April 1970	*After Magritte* presented by Inter-Action at the Green Banana Restaurant, directed by Geoffrey Reeves with Prunella Scales and Stephen Moore.
December 1970	*Where Are They Now?* broadcast by the BBC, produced by John Tydeman.
December 1971	*Dogg's Our Pet* presented by Inter-Action at the Almost Free Theatre, directed by Ed Berman.
February 1972	*Jumpers* presented by the National Theatre at the Old Vic, directed by Peter Wood with Michael Hordern and Diana Rigg.
April 1972	*After Magritte* and *The Real Inspector Hound* at the Shaw Theatre, directed by Nigel Gordon.
November 1972	*Artist Descending a Staircase* broadcast by the BBC, produced by John Tydeman.
March 1973	*Rosencrantz and Guildenstern Are Dead* revived at Young Vic, directed by Bernard Goss.
June 1974	*Travesties* presented by the RSC at the Aldwych, directed by Peter Wood with John Wood, John Hurt and Tom Bell.
August 1975	Young Vic production of *Rosencrantz and Guildenstern* transferred to Criterion.

April 1976	*Dirty Linen* and *New-Found-Land* presented by Inter-Action at the Almost Free Theatre, directed by Ed Berman with Peter Bowles, Luan Peters, Stephen Moore and Richard Goolden. The production transferred to the Arts Theatre in June.
September 1976	*Jumpers* revived at the National Theatre, directed by Peter Wood with Michael Hordern and Julie Covington.
July 1977	*Every Good Boy Deserves Favour* with music by André Previn performed by the London Symphony Orchestra conducted by André Previn, with John Wood, Ian McKellen and other actors from the RSC directed by Trevor Nunn.
September 1977	*Professional Foul* transmitted by BBC television directed by Michael Lindsay-Hogg with Peter Barkworth and John Shrapnel.

Performances of Adaptations

May 1960	*Tango* by Slawomir Mrozek, translated by Nicholas Bethell, adapted by Tom Stoppard. Presented by the RSC at the Aldwych, directed by Trevor Nunn with Peter Jeffrey and Robert Eddison.
May 1973	*The House of Bernarda Alba* by Garcia Lorca. English version by Tom Stoppard (based on a literal translation by Katie Kendall). At Greenwich Theatre, directed by Robin Phillips.
1975	*Three Men in a Boat*, BBC TV.

FIRST INTERVIEW WITH TOM STOPPARD 12 June 1974

Ronald Hayman: *Some people got the impression from* Jumpers *that you'd been a student of philosophy, and in the programme for* Travesties *you mention your indebtedness to Lenin's* Collected Works, *half a dozen books about him, an illustrated history of the First World War, two books on James Joyce and two on Dada. Obviously you make your preliminary reading almost integral to the writing.*

Tom Stoppard: That's been true right from my journalism days. A lot of my reading has resulted from the sheer necessity of having something to deliver—a piece of writing. An article on Norman Mailer for some arts page somewhere. You read the works of Norman Mailer in fourteen days in order to write an article of 1200 words. With *Jumpers* I was reading stuff I'd never have dreamed of getting round to. The books on ethics and moral philosophy that went into *Jumpers* I found immensely enjoyable. I think I enjoyed the rules that philosophers play by. It's an extremely formal discipline.

How much time do you spend reading?

I like newspapers very much. While working in journalism it became a habit to read every paper every day, and see who'd done it best. Afterwards I simply had every paper delivered to the house. Now I take *The Times, The Guardian, The Mail* and *The Mirror*. I don't usually take more than 45 minutes on them. Sometimes an hour. I don't actually move my lips when I read but I do read very slowly, and something quite definite happened to my frame of mind to do with what I wanted to read. My time for reading fiction had been spent. 'Your time is up. Come in Number 7.' Because the time I had left was only sufficient to read factual and expository, non-imaginative material. I've no desire at all to read the works of Ibsen, though I have a desire to read Michael Meyer's biography of Ibsen. I've no desire to read Kingsley Amis. I read *Lucky Jim* in 1954 and

Tom Stoppard

thoroughly enjoyed it, and haven't read a single book of his since. Why not? There's no good reason.

There's an argument about the value of art in Travesties *which is almost identical to an argument in* Artist Descending a Staircase—

If it's worth using once, it's worth using twice.

But is this an argument you have with yourself?

One of the impulses in *Travesties* is to try to sort out what my answer would in the end be if I was given enough time to think every time I'm asked why my plays aren't political, or ought they to be? Sometimes I have a complete comical reaction, and I think that in the future I must stop compromising my plays with this whiff of social application. They must be entirely untouched by any suspicion of usefulness. I should have the courage of my lack of convictions.

Structurally you seem to make more demands on yourself from one play to the next. How much do you plan in advance?

My experience is that a lot of one's work is the result of lucky accident. When you look at the body of it and see all these lucky accidents all in one go, one assumes there must be some kind of almost premeditated connection between them, but there isn't—only in so far as one might suspect the subconscious of working overtime. The plays seem to hinge around incredibly carefully thought-out structural pivots which I arrive at as thankfully and as unexpectedly as an explorer parting the pampas grass which is head-high and seeing a valley full of sunlight and maidens. No compass. Nothing.

In an ideal state all the meaningful and referential possibilities in a work of art exist in a highly compressed form in the mind of the artist, probably before he even begins, and the existence of that nucleus dictates what the tentacles do at the extremities of his conscious gift. What's wrong with bad art is that the artist knows exactly what he's doing.

When things work out well, it must look to you as though you've been lucky, but it isn't really just a matter of chance, is it?

Irving Wardle in *The Times* mentioned the reference to James Joyce's middle name being registered as Augusta as 'according to Stoppard'. He couldn't believe it really. In the play Carr says he was christened James Augustine but there was a clerical error and it came out 'James Augusta'. This in fact happens to be the case, and it's something I came across after making Joyce into Lady Bracknell, as it were. Similarly, after thinking the scheme would accommodate Tristan Tzara in the role of John Worthing, it transpired that that role was played in the Zurich production by an actor whose first name was Tristan. But this sort of thing just happens again and again and again, and on a less uncanny level it's commonplace.

When *The Real Inspector Hound* is over, and one sees that the corpse had to be Higgs, and that the chap in the wheel-chair had to be the third-string critic Puckeridge, it really seems to be a bit of Chippendale as far as all that dovetailing business goes. In fact you write away into a tunnel, you have a corpse on the floor, and you don't know who it is or what to do with him, and suddenly you say 'HIGGS!!!'. But I very seldom go into a play thinking about that kind of fairly refined analytical cross-reference structure. Obviously, the more material you have behind you, the greater the possibilities are in arithmetical progression for cross-reference and compass-point co-ordinates, as it were.

How did you arrive at the idea of making the scheme accommodate Tristan Tzara in the role of John Worthing?

It was a combination of joke for joke's sake and playwright's convenience. Obviously I'd already realized that I wanted to use the *Importance* scheme, and at the same time Tzara was a Rumanian. I can't bear the thought of an actor doing a Maurice Chevalier accent. I can't bear Maurice Chevalier. Therefore one must say, 'All right, in that case it's going to be done in perfect English, and therefore I'll put in a previous scene in which he has a French-Rumanian accent and he's monocled and ludicrous and outrageous, just to establish that'. One of the things that tickled me about the situation is that it's rather like one of those Magritte paintings in which there's a picture of a shoe, and

Tom Stoppard

underneath it's labelled 'A HORSE'. I think it's the same sort of joke when you're faced with the image of John Hurt with his perfect, eternal English languor sitting there, and someone saying to him, 'You bloody Rumanian wog!'. It's Magritte labelling, and I can't think off-hand of any more dignified intellectual credential for that aspect of the play. It's not intended to be point-making.

Jumpers seems to take its starting point from that moment in Rosencrantz and Guildenstern *when Rosencrantz says, 'Shouldn't we be doing something constructive?' and Guildenstern asks him, 'What did you have in mind? A short blunt human pyramid?'*

I did begin with that image. Speaking as a playwright—which is a category that must have its own boundary marks, because a novelist couldn't say what I'm about to say—I thought: 'How marvellous to have a pyramid of people on a stage, and a rifle shot, and one member of the pyramid just being blown out of it and the others imploding on the hole as he leaves'. I really like theatrical events, and I was in a favourable position. Because of the success of *Rosencrantz* it was on the cards that the National Theatre would do what I wrote, if I didn't completely screw it up, and it has forty, fifty actors on the pay-roll. You can actually write a play for ten gymnasts. I was in a fairly good position to indulge myself with playing around with quite complex—not to say expensive—theatrical effects and images, and I was taken with this image of the pyramid of gymnasts.

It's perfectly true that having shot this man out of the pyramid, and having him lying on the floor, I didn't know who he was or who had shot him or why or what to do with the body. Absolutely not a clue. So one worked from a curiously anti-literary starting point. You've simply committed yourself to giving nine hundred people in a big room which we call a theatre a sort of moment—yes? At the same time there's more than one point of origin for a play, and the only useful metaphor I can think of for the way I think I write my plays is convergences of different threads. Perhaps carpet-making would suggest something similar.

4

One of the threads was the entirely visual image of the pyramid of acrobats, but while thinking of that pyramid I knew I wanted to write a play about a professor of moral philosophy, and it's the work of a moment to think that there was a metaphor at work in the play already between acrobatics, mental acrobatics and so on. Actually it's not a bad way of getting excited about a play.

Somebody told me that Alfred Hitchcock has been trying to make a film which begins in a car factory in which cars are put together entirely by automation and you just dolly along these incredible gantries with mechanical arms putting wheels on, and the doors are clamped on, and at the end of this interminable process—during which the credits are rolling—down the ramp at the further end of the complex rolls this car, untouched by human hand. You open the boot and inside is a body. I'm told that as soon as he can work out how it got there he'll make the picture.

But as a playwright you can start without knowing.

Yes, that's true. Because you have other threads converging, and I suppose in the end you can just change your mind, and if you can get enough threads going for you, you can leave out the one you started with.

Did Rosencrantz and Guildenstern *feel like a breakthrough? It seems as though you suddenly got fed up with trying to entertain naturalistically and gave yourself permission to take more risks.*

I didn't, you know. All the way from *Enter a Free Man*, which was 1960, to *Travesties* (1974) I've written what appealed to me, and I've written it with the assumption that it would appeal to everybody else. It's surely true that if you don't actually write from that standpoint, you get into deep trouble.

Then what was new about Rosencrantz *?*

Four or five years had elapsed since *Enter a Free Man,* and when I was writing *Rosencrantz* I was in no sense engaged in any sort of esoteric work. It was like music-hall if anything—a slightly literate music-hall perhaps. *Enter a Free Man* was a play written

Tom Stoppard

about other people's characters. It appears to be much more about real people than *Travesties,* which is a huge artifice, but at least I've got a mental acquaintance with the characters in *Travesties,* however much, in one sense, they're two-dimensional dream people. Now *Enter a Free Man* looks as though it's about people as real—at least in terms of art—as the people in *Coronation Street.* But to me the whole thing is a bit phoney, because they're only real because I've seen them in other people's plays. I haven't actually met any of them myself. It's about upper-working-class families. They had to be a bit upper because I kept giving them extremely well-constructed speeches to speak at a high speed of knots. The main point really is that it's actually impossible to write anything at all unless you're absolutely behind it. I think that *Travesties* is capable of entertaining more people than *Enter a Free Man.* Everything I've written—at the time I've written it, I've felt 'Oh this is absolutely accessible, communicable.' To qualify that, I haven't felt that at all. One doesn't think it. One simply writes what one is impelled to write at that time, what one wants to write, what one feels one can write. Even on the single occasion when I've actually written a play for a specific occasion. I knew the boys who were going to perform it. There was one headmasterish figure that I made into a headmaster, but—all that being said—what actually emerged was something that I was absolutely behind. I was really excited by the idea of the language I was using having a double existence. One of the things I hope I'll do one day is really to make full use of that little idea I used. *Dogg's Our Pet* is an anagram of Dogg's Troupe. The play is constructed out of a vocabulary of about fifty words, all based on certain sound values.

But there must be influences. Enter a Free Man is a pre-Beckett play and Rosencrantz is obviously Beckettian. At the end of Jumpers *you actually find a way of saying thank you to him.*

At the time when *Godot* was first done, it liberated something for anybody writing plays. It redefined the minima of theatrical validity. It was as simple as that. He got away. He won by twenty-eight lengths, and he'd done it with so little—and I mean

6

hat as an enormous compliment. There we all were, busting a gut with great monologues and pyrotechnics, and this extraordinary genius just put this play together with enormous refinement, and then with two completely unprecedented and uncategorizable bursts of architecture in the middle—terrible metaphor—and there it was, theatre! So that was liberating.

It's only too obvious that there's a sort of Godotesque element in *Rosencrantz.* I'm an enormous admirer of Beckett, but if I have to look at my own stuff objectively, I'd say that the Beckett novels show as much as the plays, because there's a Beckett joke which is the funniest joke in the world to me. It appears in various forms but it consists of confident statement followed by immediate refutation by the same voice. It's a constant process of elaborate structure and sudden—and total—dismantlement. In *Travesties,* when John Wood is saying Joyce was this without being that, each sentence radically qualifies the statement before it until he ends up with 'a complex personality'. That sort of Beckettian influence is much more important to me than a mere verbal echo of a line or a parallelism at the end of *Jumpers.* That, if you like, is an open, shy bit of tribute-making, whereas the debt is rather larger than that.

There's an element of coincidence in what's usually called influence. One's appetites and predilections are obviously not unique. They overlap with those of countless other people, one of whom—praise be God—is Samuel Beckett. And it's not surprising if there are fifty writers in England who share in some way a predilection for a certain kind of intellectual or verbal humour or conceit which perhaps in some different but recognizable way is one which Beckett likes and uses.

From play to play Beckett's stage directions progressively give less freedom to the director and actors. How do you feel about that?

I think, truth be told, that were there a language one could do it in, like musical notation, I'd like to notate my plays so that there's only one way of doing everything in them. That's not to say that that would produce the best result. I know from past experience that I've been quite wrong about the way things ought to look and how lines ought to be spoken. One ought to be there for the first production and chance the rest. The first production in France of *Rosencrantz* was a nonsense and I haven't been done in France since.[1]

What about T.S. Eliot and Prufrock?

There are certain things written in English which make me feel as a diabetic must feel when the insulin goes in. Prufrock and Beckett are the twin syringes of my diet, my arterial system.

How much did you change the text of Rosencrantz *after the Edinburgh production?*

I added a scene. Laurence Olivier pointed out that the section in which they're asked by Claudius to go and find Hamlet after he's killed Polonius ought to be in the play. So I went off and wrote that. Otherwise it's the same. There was one speech that was cut at the National which went back in later, but on the whole the Edinburgh text was shorter.

Is there ever a conflict between literary and theatrical pressures?

I realized quite a long time ago that I was in it because of the theatre rather than because of the literature. I like theatre, I like showbiz, and that's what I'm true to. I really think of the theatre as valuable and I just hope very much that it'll remain like that as an institution. I think it's vital that the theatre is run by people who like showbiz. 'If a thing doesn't work, why is it there in that form?' is roughly the philosophy, and I've benefited greatly from Peter Wood's down-to-earth way of telling me, 'Right, I'm sitting in J 16, and I don't understand what you're trying to tell me. It's not clear.' There's none of this stuff about 'When Faber and Faber bring it out, I'll be able to read it six times and work it out for myself.' Too late.

What happens in practice is that after a certain number of weeks elapse I can't see the play any more. I've lost my view of

---

[1] Since the interview *Rosencrantz and Guildenstern Are Dead* has been produced successfully in Paris.

it, and I'm at the mercy of anybody who nudges me. That can work to my disadvantage because it can make the play unnecessarily broad, when I should have kept faith with the delicacy of it. At the same time, it's meant that Peter has actually saved the play. The speech in which Joyce justifies his art wasn't in the text of *Travesties* that I gave to Peter. It was he who said it was necessary, and I now think it's the most important speech in the play. It's showbiz, but the speech is there because of its place in the argument.

What about Cecily's lecture at the beginning of Act Two? Surely you're not expecting the audience to digest so much information so quickly?

There are several levels going here, and one of them is that what I personally like is the theatre of audacity. I thought, 'Right. We'll have a rollicking first act, and they'll all come back from their gin-and-tonics thinking "Isn't it fun? What a lot of lovely jokes!" And they'll sit down, and this pretty girl will start talking about the theory of Marxism and the theory of capitalism and the theory of value. And the smiles, because they're not prepared for it, will atrophy.' And that to me was like a joke in itself. But the important thing was that I'd ended the first act with what at that stage was a lengthy exposition of Dada. I wanted to begin the second with a corresponding exposition of how Lenin got to Zurich, not in geographical but political terms. I chose to do that from square one by starting from *Das Kapital*, Marxian theory of profit, theory of labour, theory of value, and then to slide into the populist movement, the terrorism, Ulyanov's brother and so on. If I could have brought that off, I'd have been prouder of that than anything else I'd ever written. There wasn't a joke in it but I felt I could get away with it because it was going to be a new set—to start with, we weren't going to begin in the library—a new character and a new scene after the interval. I overplayed that hand very badly, and at the first preview I realized that the speech had to be about Lenin only. The second act is Lenin's act really, and I just blue-pencilled everything up to the mention of Lenin. So now it was one page instead of five.

Tom Stoppard

In my original draft I took the Lenin section out of the play far more radically than in the version you saw. I actually stopped the play and had actors coming down to read that entire passage from clipboards or lecterns, because I felt very strongly—and now I believe I was right—that one thing I could not do was to integrate the Lenins into the *Importance* scheme. Irving Wardle said he'd have liked to see Lenin as Miss Prism, but that would have killed the play because of the trivialization. It would have been disastrous to Prismize and Chasublize the Lenins, and I believe that that section saves *Travesties* because I think one's just about *had* that particular Wilde joke at that point. I wanted the play to stop—to give the audience documentary illustration of what Lenin felt about art and so on, and then carry on with the play. Peter Wood's objection was unarguable: the whole thing is within the framework of Carr's memory except this bit. How do you get back people's belief if you interrupt it?

What I was trying was this. What I'm always trying to say is 'Firstly, A. Secondly, minus A.' What was supposed to be happening was that we have this rather frivolous nonsense going on, and then the Lenin section comes in and says, 'Life is too important. We can't afford the luxury of this artificial frivolity, this nonsense going on in the arts.' Then he says, 'Right. That's what I've got to say,' and he sits down. Then the play stands up and says, 'You thought *that* was frivolous? You ain't seen nothin' yet.' And you go into the Gallagher and Shean routine. That was the architectural thing I was after.

What's altered is the sympathy level you have with Lenin. When you read the words on the page there's a sense in which Lenin keeps convicting himself out of his own mouth. It's absurd. It's full of incredible syllogisms. All the publishing and libraries and bookshops and newspapers must be controlled by the Party. The press will be free. Anybody can write anything they like but anybody who uses the Party press to speak against the Party naturally won't be allowed to do it. And then you go back to the first proposition that everything's controlled by the Party, and you're going round in circles. It's sheer nonsense. And at the end he says, 'I can't listen to music. It makes you want to pat people's heads when you really have to HATE them without MERCY. Though ideally we're against doing violence to people.'

In the text one's trying to demonstrate that he was in an impossible position. The ethics of necessity syndrome was operating. But in theatrical terms Frank Windsor and Barbara Leigh Hunt are 98.4 degrees from top to bottom. They're just blood heat, they're so human. When they walk on the stage you don't really think that man has contradicted himself throughout and condemned himself out of his own mouth. You think he really had a burden to carry, and Ashkenazy is doing his bit in the loudspeaker, playing the Apassionata. The equation is different, and even I am seduced by it.

Generally speaking, are long speeches dangerous?

I always think that they're the safe parts of the play, and they've proved to be so. With *Jumpers* a certain amount of boggling went on when they saw the script. Michael Hordern was worried; Peter was worried. In practice the monologues played themselves, and all the conventionally easy bits—the dialogue—were very difficult indeed to get right. In *Travesties* John Wood, who has the grave disadvantage of being about four times as intelligent as it's good for an actor to be, came in when we were talking about the monologue and he simply said, 'I've looked at it at home. There are no problems in it.' And we didn't rehearse it—just went through it a few times when we were doing the run-throughs and I think I spent two hours with him one day talking about little details of inflection.

What about this question of increasing architectural complexity? It must have the effect of multiplying the unpredictables and the variables and the points where balance will change from one performance to the next.

Yes, I really have a deep desire not to get involved in that kind of play for a long time. It's wonderful that Peter brought *Travesties* off in theatrical terms, but it's like an egg-and-spoon race. As he says. It could have dropped off in previews at any moment. One's energy as a writer is going into *theatricality,* and

Tom Stoppard

that's okay, but one doesn't want to do that each time, and ideally what I'd like to write now is something that takes place in a whitewashed room with no music and no jumping about, but which is a literary piece—so that the energy can go into the literary side of what I do. I'd like to write a quiet play.

Jumpers and *Travesties* are very similar plays. No one's said that, but they're so similar that were I to do it a third time it would be a bore. You start with a prologue which is slightly strange. Then you have an interminable monologue which is rather funny. Then you have scenes. Then you end up with another monologue. And you have unexpected bits of music and dance, and at the same time people are playing ping-pong with various intellectual arguments.

I can see they have that in common, but the relationship between the abstract ideas and the concrete characters seems different.

Yes, and there are senses in which *Travesties* is a great advance on *Jumpers,* but it's the same kind of pig's breakfast, and I'd really like to abandon that particular paintbox and do a piece of literature for three voices and a dog. One is playing a double game with a play like *Jumpers* and *Travesties:* one is judged as a writer on the strength of what one manages to bring off theatrically, and I'm afraid, with respect to those critics whom I feel to be perceptive, that the chances of a play being judged in isolation from what is done to that play are not great. I was the beneficiary of that happening once, in the case of Ronald Bryden's review of *Rosencrantz.* The play was done in a church hall on a flat floor so that people couldn't actually see it. There was no scenery, student actors. The director didn't show up. Someone else filled in. I turned up for thirty-six hours and tried to put a few things right. It went on in some kind of state or other, and Ronald Bryden, writing for the *Observer,* just saw straight through to the text. But if Peter had got *Travesties* wrong, he would have been said to have failed as a director and I would have been said to have failed as a writer, with the same text with which Peter succeeded. It's a nonsense. There's an equation to be got right and there are a number of variables in it. It's not a question of something being right or wrong, it's a question of the variables adding up to the right answer. Things are so interrelated.

ENTER A FREE MAN

It was Stoppard himself who made the unkindest comments on his first two stage plays when he dubbed *Enter a Free Man* 'Flowering Death of a Salesman' and *The Gamblers* 'Waiting for Godot in the Condemned Cell'. *Enter a Free Man* was written in about three months during the second half of 1960 when he was twenty-three and at the end of his six-year career as a full-time journalist. He had been reviewing plays as second-string critic for the *Bristol Evening World* and, as he says[1], a first play 'tends to be the sum of all the plays you have seen of a type you can emulate technically and have admired'. Like Arthur Miller's *Death of a Salesman* (1949), Robert Bolt's *Flowering Cherry* (1957) hinges on the polarity between daydream and reality in the life of a man sacked from a dreary job. Both men are subject to delusions; both plays use these as a pretext for jumping away from the realism which is encouraged by the set.

Enter a Free Man also bears a strong resemblance to Ibsen's *The Wild Duck*, though Tom Stoppard assures me he has neither seen it nor read it. Hjalmar Ekdal is a lazy middle-aged man whose only talent is for self-deception. He talks grandly about his ambitions as an inventor and prides himself on being the breadwinner for the family, while actually depending on the earnings of his hard-working wife, her daughter Hedvig and his father. As Dr Relling explains, almost everybody needs a 'life-lie' to protect him from self-contempt and despair. Lies are as closely related to ideals, he says, as typhus is to typhoid fever. It is Relling who has convinced Hjalmar of his potential as an inventor, while Hedvig has fortified the fantasy 'with all the power and strength a child's mind is capable of'.

Enter a Free Man light-heartedly develops the theme of the life-lie without depending on solidly realized relationships

[1] Interview in *Theatre Quarterly*. See Bibliography.

between the characters. Realization of this sort could never have been Stoppard's forte and his development has carried him felicitously away from the need to depend on it. In most of his work the dazzling brightness of the comedy stops us from asking ourselves 'Is this relationship convincing?' Between 1960 and 1968 *Enter a Free Man* underwent several revisions, including a television adaptation. In the version which was finally staged in the West End, the only sequence that fails to achieve the conviction it needs is the serious conversation between the wife, Persephone, and the daughter, Linda, at the beginning of Act Two:

PERSEPHONE: I turned down one or two before your father.

LINDA: Did you? Were you ever sorry?

PERSEPHONE: What a thing to say!

LINDA: Well, were you?

PERSEPHONE: No. No, I wasn't. I knew he wasn't . . . safe, like most people are safe. But safety isn't everything. A safe man in a safe job. Well, it's not everything.

LINDA: It's money, though.

PERSEPHONE: There's lots of people like your father—different. Some make more money, because they're different. And some make none, because they're different. The difference is the thing, not the money.

LINDA: Well, that's nice, isn't it? What am I doing in a rotten shop? I could stay at home and be different. Starving but different.

The dialogue is at its worst when trying to explain relationships and at its best when demonstrating a lack of contact between two people who are having a conversation. George Riley finds his only appreciative audience in the pub, where Carmen, the barman, sympathizes without listening and Able, the gormless sailor, admires without understanding, while Harry, who lives on his bets and his wits, mocks at Riley with an irony he fails to notice:

HARRY: Don't you think George here is a clever bloke?

ABLE: 'Course he's a clever bloke. He's an inventor, isn't he?

15

Tom Stoppard

HARRY: My very point. An inventor. That's your job. Amazing. I don't know if you've ever thought, George, but if you took away everything in the world that had to be invented, there's be nothing left except a lot of people getting rained on.

RILEY *(excitedly)*: You're right! Progress is the child of invention! . . . *(Soberly)* Harry, I have been touched by what you have said.

At home there is no one to sympathize with George. Persephone has heard it all too many times; Linda is undeceived by the meticulous accounts he keeps of the pocket money she lends him out of her weekly salary from Woolworth's. George is foolish enough to build his plans for the future on Harry's offer of a partnership, a comic balloon which will obviously be pricked at their next meeting.

Another layer is added to the build-up towards disaster when Florence arrives at the pub just too late to meet Harry. Obvious though it is that she is his girl, George, with his genius for one-sided conversations, convinces himself that she will give him the appreciation he can no longer get from Persephone:

RILEY: Florence, you and I—we've been wasted. It has taken me years to make the break because I have always been alone . . . But for you, Florence, it need not be like that, if there is someone beside you. Florence, I am . . . old . . . *(he looks at her carefully but there is no contradiction)* . . . no longer handsome, features that are perhaps more interesting than beautiful . . . *(Pause)*

FLORENCE: I should think you were quite good-looking when you were young.

RILEY: I was, I was! Technically, I have made the break. *(He rises and strides away from the table)* I shall go back this evening, I suppose—well just to gather a few things, and tomorrow will see me in this spot. I'm meeting my partner—I have a partner, you know. There'll be a few details to settle and then the sky's the limit. And now you, whom destiny has cast in this shabby place at this golden moment—in you I see a fellow spirit.

He has made so many previous attempts to leave home that Persephone no longer takes them seriously: she goes on laying his place at the dinner table. Obviously his life-lie will be punctured by the simultaneous discovery that Florence is mainly interested in Harry and Harry not at all interested in becoming his partner; but his self-esteem is rubbery enough for such punctures to be repaired easily. As Stoppard puts it in a stage direction, he is 'unsinkable despite the slow leak'. The climacteric sequence is by no means ineffective, but the comedy and the bids for sympathy are not working comfortably together. Before leaving with Florence, Harry points out that Riley is depending on an idea that won't work: an envelope with gum on both sides of the flap cannot be used twice because it will be torn after it has been opened once.

> RILEY: Ah yes, yes . . . Yes, I think he's got a point, you know. How very extraordinary. *(Turning to* CARMEN *who is in sympathetic attendance)* The fact is, it was not a very *practical* idea, though it did have a certain . . . flair . . .
> CARMEN: Oh yes, Mr Riley, it had a lot of flair.
> RILEY: But not practical.
> CARMEN: A bit impractical, yes. Ahead of its time.
> RILEY: Is that it?—is that it? Yes—well, of course the public isn't ready—that's true, they go around ripping envelopes to shreds . . .
> CARMEN: That's just about it, Mr Riley.
> RILEY *(going to door and gathering up his things)*: Quite. Well, never mind, never mind—I've got a few shots left in my locker, oh my goodness yes—let's see there's my, er . . . my . . .
> ABLE*'s laugh starts coming through loud and clear*
> ABLE *(laughing)*: You didn't even know his name . . .
> RILEY *is hurt to anguish, turns and leaves.*

The action is on safer ground when it stays close to farce. It is very amusing when Riley mistakes a charmless man in the pub for an industrial spy intent on stealing his secrets:

> ABLE: We'll have to break down his cover.

Tom Stoppard

BROWN: I assure you—

ABLE *(excitedly)*: Maybe he's got the place bugged!

BROWN: I really—

ABLE: Microphones! Look for secret microphones! *(Snatches the man's buttonhole and tosses it aside. Looks under the table)*

BROWN: Stop it—how dare you!

ABLE: Destroy the tapes!

RILEY: Out with it, Smith!

BROWN: Brown.

RILEY: Give me that tape.

BROWN *(shrill)*: Leave me alone!

RILEY *(calmly decisive)* : All right. *(Murmurs to* ABLE*)* Give me the cigarettes. Psychology. Picked it up in the war. *(He becomes friendly)* Cigarette?

Stoppard is already showing talent for developing extravagant ideas into lively action.

The construction benefits from having both the house and the pub represented on the set—an idea that appears to have been evolved out of a question which is posed in intellectual terms before being answered in theatrical terms. Linda is wondering whether Riley presents the same personality in the pub as he does at home. Stoppard then lets us see the answer for ourselves as Riley makes his entrance in the pub, announcing himself with a fanfare that already sounds off-key. 'Enter a free man!' The dialogue from the other locale overlaps: 'Poor old Dad,' says Linda. 'It's him again,' says Harry. Even in the pub they have heard it all before.

Later Stoppard will devise more sophisticated methods of exploring the dilemma of the ordinary man caught up with extraordinary people and extraordinary events. This is what Rosencrantz, Guildenstern and Henry Carr (in *Travesties*) have in common. They are funnily and pathetically out of their depth. So is George Moore in *Jumpers*: he is just an ordinary moral philosopher. As Stoppard says[1], he could equally well have been

---

[1] Interview with Mark Amory in the *Observer Magazine*. See Bibliography.

a playwright or a vicar. In *Enter a Free Man* the only extraordinary element is the grandiosity of Riley's life-lie. He is otherwise an ordinary man in an ordinary situation, and he is never more touching than when verging on awareness of this:

> My wife and I and Linda, we get up in the morning and the water is cold . . . fried bread and sausage and tea . . . the steam in the kitchen and the smell of it all and the springs are broken in my chair . . . Linda goes to sell things . . . in Woolworth's . . . cosmetics and toilet things, and we wash up when the kettle boils again . . . and I go to my room . . . and sit there . . . with my pencils and my workbench . . . I've got a workbench, you know . . . and sit there . . . The Hoover is on HP, Linda got it, she pays for it every Friday and it drones all morning . . . like an aeroplane in the house but far away . . . flying from room to room far away, and the doors open and close so many times . . . we've only got seven doors, but they open and close all the time . . .

This is part of a long speech which is made to seem shorter than it is by starting in the pub and ending in the home. As he talks, Riley moves away to lean against a table in the centre of the set, where a spotlight picks him out while the lights cross-fade between the two locales. This anti-naturalistic gesture has its effect, but the main theatrical energy is in the verbal inventiveness. Throughout the play, each new idea leads into cadenzas of comic fantasy. Even Riley's humourlessness becomes an asset:

> RILEY *(with scorn)*: Dreams! The illusion of something for nothing. No wonder the country is going to the dogs. Personal enterprise sacrificed to bureaucracy. No pride, no patriotism. The erosion of standards, the spread of mediocrity, the decline of craftsmanship and the betrayal of the small inventor.

And, with Able as his accomplice, Riley inflates his suspicion that Brown is an industrial spy until the pub has become an imaginary courtroom with Riley as Q.C.

Tom Stoppard

RILEY: Now look here; I don't care if your name is Smith or Jones or Robinson. I don't care if your father was a mermaid or a sea lion or even your father. The question is—*what are you playing at*?

CARMEN: Mr Riley, I'll ask you—

RILEY: Silence in the public gallery! Now for the last time—and remember you're on oath—I ask you in all solemnity—and think carefully before you reply—I ask you—God dammit, now I've forgotten the question—I wish you'd all keep quiet!

Other characters are given something of the same capacity for self-absorption. Not even noticing Able's gauche attempts to pick her up, Florence muses wistfully about the film she was nearly in, until Riley, with equal gaucheness, leads her masterfully away.

The construction is very neat. At the end of Act One the dialogue loops back to the sequence we heard earlier on as Riley arrived at the pub. The end of the second act nearly echoes the dialogue we heard last time Linda was lending her father money, which is what she is again doing. There is also something of a visual climax when a thunderstorm activates the invention of Riley's which has been visible on the set—pipes eccentrically ducted into the living room to let the indoor plants benefit from the rain. There is no means of checking the flow of water, so Linda has to fetch buckets and saucepans.

Three Stories
REUNION,
LIFE, TIMES: FRAGMENTS
and THE STORY

In 1964 Faber and Faber published *Introduction 2: Stories by New Writers*, forecasting in the preface that the five authors all stood 'a very reasonable chance of establishing themselves among the more interesting novelists of the future'. The confidence they felt in Stoppard is understandable. His novel *Lord Malquist and Mr Moon* (1966) deserves more attention than it has had, and his three stories, which were written in 1963, are extremely lively.

Unlike most of his later work, they are often overtly auto-biographical and they are not consistently leavened with comedy. 'Reunion' is reminiscent of the early Eliot poems which wryly describe encounters with women who would have preferred the conversation not to fall so far short of the romantic. Without ever lapsing into facile romanticism, Stoppard's narrative seems to be aiming at more detachment than it can achieve while dividing its focus between the man's vertiginous instability and his self-pity. An act of violence, like smashing a bottle of milk against the kitchen sink, would save him, momentarily, from the need that will suck him back into the adulterous affair.

Instead of determining the structural progression, as they do in the plays, jokes and fantasies are merely part of the conversation. At first the woman says her husband will be back soon; later she allows herself to be wooed into submissiveness by his bravura in developing the notion that there is a certain word 'which if shouted at the right pitch and in a silence worthy of it, would nudge the universe into gear . . . All the things which just miss will just click right, and the mind that heaves and pops like boiling porridge will level off, secretly'. Her resistance is broken, decisively, by his story of knocking a prayer-book off a ledge in the middle of a two-minute silence: 'It hit the floor flat and went off like a pistol shot. I reckon for two seconds

21

everything intrusive to my self flew out of me, and then back.' The climacteric love-making is described deftly, wittily, and the story's economy—it is scarcely more than four pages long—both pegs back the self-indulgence and conveys an impression of precision.

The other stories are both about working as a journalist. 'Life, Times: Fragments', which swerves eccentrically between anecdote and parody (of Eliot's *Prufrock*) contains an account of applying for a job on the *Evening Standard* and being interviewed by the editor:

> What are your special interests? he asked. Well ah reading. The editor seemed to think his question had been misunderstood. Interested in politics at all? Oh yes, indeed, politics, too. Who then, for instance, was the Foreign Secretary?

Walking down Fleet Street, the rejected journalist decides that the question had been unfair.

The most piquant foretaste of the later work comes in the use of a spiky pun to puncture a ballooning literary conceit. He lectures his girl friend with a scornful dismissal of Flaubert, Stendhal, Henry James, Wilde, Thackeray, Tolstoy, Turgenev, Proust, Lawrence, Scott Fitzgerald and Hemingway. The models are no good any more, he tells her. We've had all that. We're on our own now. Gathering confidence from his own rhetoric and 'hoarse with carnage' he boasts

> 'I will do it, yes, that much I know, I will do it and it will be for you,' and, wild, shameless, whispered the urgent unspeakable secret, '*I am—I feel—seminal!*' and she, getting up, faceless for the dark, said, 'No, do you mind if we don't tonight. I've run out of the stuff.'

The Stoppard who appears in these pages is partly a fiction, partly a fact. He dramatizes his awareness of losing time without making enough headway in his career, and, as if to apologize for the strength of his compulsion to achieve success, he makes it into a subject of mockery:

the further he got from publication the closer he got to God, until the two appeared to present themselves as alternatives . . . and for a long time he compromised by praying at his typewriter.

But after receiving 127 consecutive rejection slips, he offers to cast aside his worldly ambitions and devote himself exclusively to God.

And the Lord heard him and He sent an angel to the writer as he knelt, and the angel said, 'The Lord thanks you for your contribution but regrets that it is not quite suitable for the Kingdom of Heaven'.

'The Story' is fairly conversational in manner but not at all jokey. This time the narrator is given a name, Jack, but whether the episode tallies with Stoppard's experience exactly, approximately, or not at all, he obviously shares the guilty feeling that in living by telling tales on other individuals, the reporter is often destructive and sometimes murderous. The story that gives Stoppard's story its title is one that Jack picks up in an out-of-town lawcourt, where there is only one other reporter, a junior. A thirty-eight-year-old schoolmaster from 'one of the top schools' is fined £25 for indecently touching a seven-year-old girl while teaching her to swim. After assuring the man that nothing about the case will appear in print, Jack lets himself be persuaded to feed the facts into several press pipelines, with the result that the story is spread over the national dailies. Jack earns only £3.2.6 but the teacher throws himself under a train.

The First Two Radio Plays
THE DISSOLUTION OF DOMINIC BOOT and 'M' IS FOR MOON AMONG OTHER THINGS

In comparison with the stories, these two fifteen-minute radio plays may seem lightweight, but an alert observer of form would have noticed that Stoppard's use of the medium was healthily and intelligently exploratory. Having been commissioned to write for Radio 4, he exploited all the freedoms he was being offered, creating two small dramas that could never have been presented satisfactorily in the theatre. In both, voices and sound effects make an impact which is all the greater for the audience's inability to see what is going on.

Both concepts are ambitious but simple enough for their potential to be developed fully within the time-span. The voices of Dominic and his fiancée immediately tell us a good deal about them. He is young, weak, well-meaning and expensively educated. When he talks about money, he sounds well-versed in the technique of using charm to reassure creditors that they will not have to wait long. Vivian has the loud, demanding, slightly enervating voice of the sub-débutante who will resort to bullying her man as soon as persuasion fails. The main incident is a taxi-ride which is comically prolonged when Dominic, after dropping her off, travels from point to point with mounting desperation, trying to raise money to pay the mounting fare. London taxis provide fruitily distinctive noises—the loud diesel tone of the idling engine, the characteristic door-slam and, with a little licence, the relentless ticking of the meter can be amplified menacingly in proportion to the victim's growing anxiety about the fare.

The writing is crisp, bright and economical. One line of dialogue can be enough to create a lively caricature. Taking advantage of Dominic's taxi on her way to the hairdresser, his mother says, 'I'm thinking of going blue. And piled on top'. We learn a lot about his father from the line, 'Bates, give this half crown to the taxi driver and bring us some whisky. Well now, Dominic, how's the job?'

That so many contrasted incidents are crowded, with no sense of strain, into fifteen minutes is due to very skilful cutting. As soon as his mother has said, 'I was getting quite tired of you always coming to me for money', that hope has faded and he is borrowing fourpence to ring his friend Charlie. As soon as he has lost his temper with Vivian ('Oh you stupid bitch, shut up and lend me ten pounds for the love of God') we hear him in the episode in which he is trying to sell the engagement ring to Lemon. We can guess what has happened in between.

Even within the fifteen-minute span, Stoppard is able to loop back neatly to earlier incidents. Dominic uses a poker to break his gas meter open and finds only 10/6 inside. Later the taxi-driver, who is now calling him Dominic, is in the middle of offering 10/- for his desk and 10/- for his mirror when he says: 'Somebody's bust up your gas meter'.

The neatest loop of all is the conclusive one, which carries us back to the opening. Having sold his suit, Dominic is left with nothing to wear except pyjamas and a raincoat. Returning to his office he finds himself face-to-face with the formidable Mr Cartwright. 'I'm giving you a week's notice and stop crying.' The secretary, Miss Bligh, is more sympathetic. She admires his pyjamas and hails a taxi. 'Come on, you can drop me off.'

The second play, *'M' Is for Moon among Other Things*, was worked up out of a short story which Faber and Faber had not wanted. It would be unstageable not because there is too much movement from place to place but because there is too little movement of any kind except inside the characters' minds. A middle-aged, middle-class husband and wife, Alfred and Constance, are sitting at home. He is reading a newspaper; she is reading the latest instalment of her mail-order encyclopaedia. Daydreams are prompted by what they read, so the dialogue moves between self-absorbed monologues which represent their private thoughts and the bursts of casual conversation which involve very much less of their real emotions.

ALFRED *(thinks)*: 'I found her to be a smooth-as-silk beauty with the classic lines and thrust of . . .'

25

Tom Stoppard

CONSTANCE: Alfred, is it the fifth or the sixth?

ALFRED: Mmm? *(Thinks)* '. . . surging to sixty m.p.h. in twenty-nine seconds . . .'

CONSTANCE: Fifth?

ALFRED: Fifth what?

CONSTANCE: What's today?

ALFRED: Sunday . . . *(Thinks)* . . . 'the handbrake a touch stiff and I'd like to see an extra ashtray for the passenger but otherwise . . .' *(Up)* Oh for goodness sake—you know I hate people looking over my shoulder. *(Turns page)*

CONSTANCE *(thinks)*: August the fifth, nineteen sixty-two. *(Up)* Alfred, in half an hour I'll be exactly forty-two-and-a-half years old. That's a thought, isn't it?

Like the narrator in 'Life, Times: Fragments' she is unhappy at having so little to show for the quantity of time that has passed.

Turning on the television to catch the news at five past ten, Alfred finds that *Dial M for Murder* is just finishing. The title reminds Constance that she used to be called by her middle name, Millie, and the first item on the news programme is about the death of Marilyn Monroe. Earlier, flipping through pages in the encyclopaedia and reading out the titles of articles, Constance has got as far as Molluscs, but the only Monroe to qualify for entry had been James, President of the United States. Constance's grasshopper mind jumps to her childhood ABC book:

> Everything was so simple then. I thought that each letter only stood for the one word they gave, you know? A is for Apple, B is for Baby, C is for Cat . . . M was for Moon. It was ages before I knew that M was for anything else.

Today her life is complicated by such problems as her husband's chief accountant's Catholic wife's annoyance at being offered meat when invited to dinner on a Friday:

> *(Thinks)* Oh God, if I'd been in her place I would have eaten the bloody meat and gone to confession . . . Bitch . . . I

shouldn't have phoned Alfred at the office, though . . .

He, meanwhile, is thinking about a relationship he never had:

> Marilyn . . . don't worry, I'm glad you phoned . . . Don't
> be unhappy, love, tell me all about it and I'm sure I'll think
> of something . . . Do you feel better already?—Well, it's
> nice to have someone you know you can count on any time,
> isn't it?

THE GAMBLERS

'My "first" play—that is the first play I regard as *mine*, after I'd cleared the decks with *A Walk on the Water* (*Enter a Free Man*)' is how Stoppard characterizes *The Gamblers* in his *Theatre Quarterly* interview. He also describes a meeting 'about that time' with Margaret Ramsay, the agent. 'She said, knowing nothing about *The Gamblers*, that all young writers seemed to be writing first plays about people in condemned cells.'

As the action opens, the prisoner is pessimistically considering the chances that God will send an angel, as he did to Peter when he was imprisoned by Herod. This sequence is at first reminiscent of the prayer at the typewriter in 'Life, Times: Fragments', but it soon becomes more reminiscent of *Waiting for Godot* as deliberately literary dialogue cuts against clownish stage business. The jailer, who cannot make the key work from outside the cell, is not supposed to take it off his belt. At the risk of making his trousers fall down, he takes off his belt, handing it through the grille to the prisoner, who lets him in. The role-reversal in the play also suggests an affinity with the Genet of *Deathwatch* and *The Balcony*: the prisoner used to be the jailer, but he joined the revolutionaries. Had the revolution succeeded he would now be a hero, while the present jailer, who used to be the public hangman, would have been a prisoner.

The suspense created by the imminence of the execution is un-Beckettian, but the conversation about the menu for the final meal is elaborated in the manner of a music-hall routine. Left alone, the prisoner moves on to a different rhetorical plane:

> Revolution from a distance, detached, noises on the wind and from time to time the drum of whipped horses on the road as headless riders plunge through . . . In the capital revolution is a roar and a tide and fire and fists and pickpockets and old men's boots and bottles thrown by gumsore widows . . . Opportunity for whores and

heroes . . . Hedges of brown and broken teeth, and running blind as brooms until the taste of pebbles in your mouth.

Then, without ceasing to be lyrical, he tried to let the wind out of his own lyricism:

Poetry, or something very like it. Well. It wasn't like that here. Villages and small towns do not precipitate changes: we are merely inheritors. So we waited, and no children played. It was just like that. You knew it was coming, for days, and then it came and you got on your horse, as usual, and then it was too late. That was yesterday.

Working towards a climax in which the two nameless men will exchange roles, Stoppard soon has to start characterizing the executioner as being attracted by the idea of martyrdom: 'The only heroes left are the leaders and the martyrs. Either way there's glory, but a martyr's lasts longer'. The build-up by means of argument is not very convincing. Stoppard is more persuasive with his comic demonstrations. In eating the condemned man's last supper, the executioner is unwillingly preparing himself for his new role as victim. Stoppard also tries to shift the discussion about martyrdom into a comic key:

Do you know what I wanted to be when I was a little boy? *(Very simply)* Joan of Arc.

The second act takes us into the morning of the execution. A crowd has gathered outside the prison. One onlooker is carrying a placard which says, 'This is only the beginning', while the contradictions in the executioner's rhetoric prefigure those of Lenin in *Travesties*:

JAILER: You are the sun on the horizon. *(Consciously theatrical)* . . . The sun of hope and truth about to flood a golden land of equality and fraternity—and—and—
PRISONER: Liberty.
JAILER: Liberty! Yes! A golden land where liberty is—*compulsory*!

Again the conversation becomes theological:

29

Tom Stoppard

JAILER: He works in mysterious ways. Our kind of justice is not . . . *mysterious* enough for him.

PRISONER: I think you may have stumbled across the definition of divine will—an obsession with mystery.

They conduct a practical experiment in the effort to make contact with God. Agreeing that the right direction for a search is upwards, they rearrange the furniture to let the prisoner climb as high as possible in the cell. He even stands on the jailer's back. Receiving no answer, he forces the jailer to stand on his:

PRISONER: Where's your sense of Evangelism?

JAILER: I don't know.

PRISONER: *Find it.*

JAILER *(frenzy, a shriek)*: *But suppose he answers!*

The final argument about their role-reversal touches on two questions that will be central in both *Rosencrantz and Guildenstern Are Dead* and *Lord Malquist and Mr Moon*: do leaders really take initiative? What is their relationship to the led? Those who appear to be the heroes may have been no more than spectators or supporters:

PRISONER *(lightly)*: I was more in the nature of rank and file. A new recruit . . . The state promoted me after the event—I didn't earn it. I forgot to tell you, I'm a coward too. But a little retrospective promotion is a useful thing. It makes the capture more impressive. It's the normal practice. They wanted to make an example of me. The real leaders took to strategic flight the moment the tide turned, or alternatively produced State flags and cheered on the militia who had come to kill them. In either case they showed a presence of mind unlooked for in that disgusting assembly of flea-ridden agitators. I had very little to do with the sordid business.

The significance of the title is explained in the prisoner's long speech about revolution. You have to back one side or the other to win, but there is no reason for preferring one to the other:

They're two parts of the same wheel, and the wheel spins.

Do you know what I mean? I mean that our insecure President who has just been so nearly deposed by one popular uprising achieved his position by a similar one seven years ago . . . The life cycle of government, from the popular to the unpopular. The wheel goes slowly round till you get back to the starting point, and it's time for another revolution.

The jailer has to recognize that this is not a man who deserves to die the glorious death of a martyr. Even when he is given the chance to run for it, he does not dare. All he can do is argue. But Stoppard is patently imposing a pattern in continuing the argument until the prisoner is wearing the executioner's mask and the jailer is ready to die, wearing the condemned man's hood. The crowd will have no means of knowing which is which.

ROSENCRANTZ AND GUILDENSTERN ARE DEAD

The germ of the idea for *Rosencrantz and Guildenstern Are Dead* was provided by Stoppard's agent, Kenneth Ewing, who had often wondered who was the King of England when Rosencrantz and Guildenstern arrived with Hamlet. If the choice had to be based on Shakespeare's other plays, it would be between King Lear and Cymbeline. What if the boat from Denmark docked at Dover while Lear was careering madly about the heath?

After *'M' Is for Moon among Other Things* had been broadcast in April 1964, Stoppard left in May to spend five months in Berlin as guest of the Ford Foundation, which had invited half a dozen young playwrights to a colloquium. They were given comfortable accommodation, good meals and plenty of time for working. Stoppard wrote *Rosencrantz and Guildenstern Meet King Lear* as a one-act verse burlesque. He had been aware from the beginning that it would be virtually impossible to write lines for King Lear or for any major Shakespearian character. Arriving at Dover and enquiring for the King, Rosencrantz and Guildenstern are informed that there are three rivals for the throne. When the mad Lear makes his appearance, he speaks lines from Shakespeare's play. Charles Marowitz, who had been asked to adjudicate at the performances and report on them for *The Times*, considered Stoppard's piece to be 'a lot of academic twaddle'; Martin Esslin, also adjudicating, was less dismissive.

Rewriting his script, Stoppard eliminated both King Lear and the action set in England, concentrating on the earlier events at Elsinore. He translated his own verse into prose, achieving a crisper contrast with Shakespeare's verse. He kept some of the original dialogue and stage-business, including the coin-tossing, and he lengthened the play into two acts. In the middle of 1965 the RSC bought an option on his new script, but at the end of twelve months it was still unproduced. It was then offered to the Oxford Playhouse and eventually passed on to the Oxford undergraduates who presented it on the fringe of the Edinburgh festival. After Ronald Bryden's enthusiastic review in *The Observer*, Kenneth Tynan asked Kenneth Ewing to send him a script to consider for the National Theatre; within six months the play was in rehearsal.

It revealed a unique blend of originality and inspired eclecticism. Clearly, Rosencrantz and Guildenstern have been wooed out from the shadow of *Godot* by 'The Lovesong of J. Alfred Prufrock':

> No! I am not Prince Hamlet, nor was meant to be;
> Am an attendant lord, one that will do
> To swell a progress, start a scene or two,
> Advise the prince; no doubt, an easy tool,
> Deferential, glad to be of use,
> Politic, cautious, and meticulous;
> Full of high sentence, but a bit obtuse;
> At times, indeed, almost ridiculous—
> Almost, at times, the Fool.

Like Vladimir and Estragon, Rosencrantz and Guildenstern could be described as figures who act out their author's *Angst* about the human condition, but Stoppard is considerably less *Angst*-ridden than Beckett, and more inclined to take his bearings from existing literature and existing cultural trends. He was fortunate enough to launch *Rosencrantz and Guildenstern* on the tide that was ebbing away from the heroic mode. It had not been until the middle fifties that the influences of Brecht and Beckett had merged in England to produce a violent reaction against the well-born, well-educated young heroes of Noël Coward and Terence Rattigan, personified by well-dressed, well-spoken young actors. In 1962 the RSC production of *The Wars of the Roses* adapted Brechtian production techniques to Shakespeare, humanizing the elements which in a fifties production would have been used as mere decoration. Instead of composing the soldiers and minor courtiers into picturesque groupings around the central heroic figure, Peter Hall and his co-directors found ways of exposing the underside of the supporting characters' theatrical existence. The audience was persuaded to sympathize with the ordinary soldiers in their physical exertions, their boredom, their despondency. In 1965, while Tom Stoppard was reworking his script of *Rosencrantz and Guildenstern*, David Warner was appearing at Stratford-on-Avon in Peter Hall's production of *Hamlet* without a princely prince. Nobility was no longer the keynote. As Ronald Bryden wrote, 'He slops ostentatiously through the castle in a greenish, moth-eaten student's gown, peering owlishly over his spectacles to cheek his elders. He knows his position as heir to the throne protects him, and abuses it as far as he can'. Or as David Warner said later in a *Times* interview, 'How the hell do I know what *princely* is? . . . You can be a prince and you can pick your nose because the prince has the freedom to do whatever he wants'.

By 1966 the public was ready for a departure from the mould of working-class anti-hero that John Osborne had established in 1956 with Jimmy Porter. Stoppard appeared at the right moment with his beautifully engineered device for propelling two attendant lords into the foreground, while Hamlet (instead of being de-nobilized) became a minor character. Stoppard was not the first playwright to incorporate generous slabs of Shakespearian dialogue into a modern text, but he was the boldest and the cleverest. More important, he was the most proficient at using the theatrical situation as an image of the human condition. Birth, growth and death come to seem like the fatalistic web of text that holds the actor stuck. Brightly coloured wings can do nothing but flutter. Stoppard generates an extra resonance for his central conceit by using the company of actors within the play as a means of connecting the Shakespearian tragedy with the new comedy that occurs in the margin. The attendant lords exist at the edge of great events they cannot control. Shakespeare, whose sympathy for Rosencrantz and Guildenstern is limited, provides little information about them; Stoppard leaves us in equal ignorance about their past lives but he focuses on their ignorance and their impotence: 'They are told very little about what is going on and much of what they are told isn't true. So I see them much more clearly as a couple of bewildered innocents rather than a couple of henchmen'. He also sympathizes profoundly with the difficulty they must have had in sitting around with so little to do.

In *The Gamblers* the explanation of the title came near the end; *Rosencrantz and Guildenstern* begins with a gambling sequence, which introduces the recurrent themes of chance, time and divine intervention. Guildenstern speculates why tossed coins should come down *heads* eighty-nine times in succession:

GUIL: One: I'm willing it. Inside where nothing shows, I am the essence of a man spinning double-headed coins, and betting against himself in private atonement for an unremembered past. *(He spins a coin at* ROS.*)*

ROS: Heads.

GUIL: Two: time has stopped dead, and the single experience of one coin being spun once has been repeated ninety times . . . *(He flips a coin, looks at it, tosses it to* ROS.*)*

John Stride (left) as Rosencrantz and Edward Petherbridge (right) as Guildenstern in the National Theatre production of *Rosencrantz and Guildenstern Are Dead.*

On the whole, doubtful. Three: divine intervention, that is to say, a good turn from above concerning him, cf. children of Israel, or retribution from above concerning me, cf. Lot's wife.

As in *Godot*, the act of waiting is a contradictory combination of doing something and doing nothing. Time may seem to have stopped but one is more aware of it than usual because there is no distracting action except the trivial actions of coin-tossing or idle conversation, which are devised, as we say, 'to pass the time'—a phrase which itself offers an illusion of control. Stoppard may seem to be 'using' Beckett, but he is also using himself—acquainting himself with his unambitious characters by inverting his own unwillingness to let time pass without making headway:

> ROS: What do you want to do?
> GUIL: I have no desires. None.

They depend on other people, external stimuli:

> We have not been . . . picked out . . . simply to be abandoned . . . set loose to find our own way . . . We are entitled to some direction . . . I would have thought.

Like Vladimir and Estragon, Rosencrantz and Guildenstern are not free simply to go away. Both pairs are on stage for almost the whole duration of the action. Vladimir and Estragon are waiting for Godot; Rosencrantz and Guildenstern have been under orders since a royal messenger woke them by banging on their shutter. Like Beckett, Stoppard uses the fact of enforced passivity as a trampoline for conversational bounces which are both energetic and entertaining. Neither dramatist heats up his characterization in the pressure-cooker of a suspenseful story. Instead the male couples are given space and leisure to broach abstruse philosophical questions against a counterpoint of slapstick activity. Beckett had shown that theatrical action could be created amusingly out of inaction. Deprived of strong motivation and of momentum, the actors have to reveal more of their own personality, but they also have more freedom to play directly to the audience, like comedians.

It is clever to bring on the troupe of players before Rosencrantz and Guildenstern meet any of the other characters from Shakespeare's play and it is apt that these specialists in illusion are introduced just after Guildenstern's story about the unicorn. The man who notices a unicorn can explain it as an illusion until a second man remarks on it. The experience is now as alarming as it can be. 'A third witness, you understand, adds no further dimension but only spreads it thinner, and a fourth thinner still, and the more witnesses there are, the thinner it gets and the more reasonable it becomes until it is as thin as reality, the name we give to the common experience.'

Stoppard does not want his tragedians to belong exclusively to any recognizable time or place, although there is a reference to the companies of boy actors that were providing vulgar competition to their seniors in Elizabethan London. Stoppard also uses an ancient joke which is not ancient enough not to be anachronistic: 'Don't clap too loudly,' says the Player, 'it's a very old world.' We are at the opposite pole from the brave new world that Miranda discovers so delightedly in *The Tempest*. The times are bad and actors have to prostitute themselves to eke out a living.

> We'll stoop to anything if that's your bent . . . *(He regards* ROS *meaningfully but* ROS *returns the stare blankly.)*

Stoppard can also comment on what he is himself doing when he makes the Player explain the 'performances' at which the audiences 'get caught up in the action':

> We keep to our usual stuff, more or less, only inside out. We do on stage the things that are supposed to happen off. Which is a kind of integrity, if you look on every exit being an entrance somewhere else.

Rosencrantz and Guildenstern is like a pocket pulled inside out to show the seams. In Anouilh's backstage drama *Colombe* we see a performance in progress as if we were looking at it from upstage; Stoppard's rearrangement of the normal perspective is subtler and more purposeful. Sometimes we feel as if we were in the wings with two small-part actors who spend most of the evening waiting for their next entrance; sometimes we feel caught up with them in the action; sometimes we feel like Alice in Wonderland, suddenly small enough to be taken on a guided tour of the pocket.

Stoppard contrives very deft transitions into Shakespeare's text. The first comes immediately after the first coin is discovered to have come down *tails*. There is a change of lighting as Ophelia runs on, pursued by Hamlet with his clothes in disarray. Stoppard's stage direction is culled directly out of Shakespeare's dialogue. In Stoppard's scene neither Hamlet nor she speaks; as soon as they have left the stage, Guildenstern says, 'Come on' to the bemused Rosencrantz, but too late. A fanfare announces the entrance of Claudius and Gertrude. Shakespeare's play has taken over. Our actors are suddenly on duty, being briefed by the King in blank verse. They reply formally, promising obedience. The excerpt is long enough for the return of twentieth-century language to give us a sickening feeling in the stomach, as when a lift lurches into rapid descent. Like Constance in *'M' Is for Moon*, they both think nostalgically of the time when everything seemed simple:

> ROS: There were answers everywhere you *looked*. There was no question about it—people knew who I was and if they didn't they asked and I told them.
>
> GUIL: You did, the trouble is, each of them is . . . plausible, without being instinctive. All your life you live so close to truth, it becomes a permanent blur in the corner of your eye, and when something nudges it into outline it is like being ambushed by a grotesque.

They try, as Vladimir and Estragon do, to cheer each other up:

> GUIL: Your smallest action sets off another somewhere else, and is set off by it. Keep an eye open, an ear cocked. Tread warily, follow instructions. We'll be all right.
>
> ROS: For how long?
>
> GUIL: Till events have played themselves out. There's a logic at work—it's all done for you, don't worry. Enjoy it.

Relax. To be taken in hand and led, like being a child again, even without the innocence, a child—It's like being given a prize, an extra slice of childhood when you least expect it, as a prize for being good, or compensation for never having had one . . . Do I contradict myself?

ROS: I can't remember . . . What have we got to go on?

GUIL: We have been briefed.

Beckett had broken the unwritten law about making his actors pretend to be ignorant of the audience's presence; in *Rosencrantz and Guildenstern*, which is more directly a play about the theatrical situation, Stoppard can go further. There is a moment at which the action stops. At the end of the hiatus Rosencrantz is staring into the audience:

ROS: How very intriguing! *(Turns)* I feel like a spectator—an appalling business. The only thing that makes it bearable is the irrational belief that somebody interesting will come on in a minute . . .

GUIL: See anyone?

ROS: No. You?

GUIL: No. *(At footlights)* What a fine persecution—to be kept intrigued without ever quite being enlightened.

Eventually they are swept up again in Shakespeare's play as they have their first conversation with Hamlet, an animated conversation overtaken by rising music and fading light as the first act ends.

Already, within thirty pages of dialogue, Stoppard has fabricated an immensely complicated pattern. According to John Wood, who played Guildenstern in New York, Stoppard's plays 'are a good deal more difficult than we think: I rehearsed *Rosencrantz and Guildenstern* for six weeks, toured for three and played for three months before I was able to hold the whole pattern in my head at once'. To understand it we have to form an impression both of the overall architecture and of the moment-to-moment progression, which is almost dialectical. Stoppard has said[1] that Rosencrantz and Guildenstern add up to

---

[1]   In the interview with Giles Gordon, see Bibliography.

him, 'in the sense that they're carrying out a dialogue which I carry out with myself. One of them is fairly intellectual, fairly incisive; the other one is thicker, nicer in a curious way, more sympathetic. There's a leader and the led'. Or as he put it in another interview[2]:

> My plays are actually constructed out of people deflating each other. I am a very hedgy sort of writer. What I think of as being my distinguishing mark is an absolute lack of certainty about almost anything. So I tend to write about oppositions, rather than heroes, don't I? I don't feel certain enough about anything to put up a hero to say it for me.

One of the reasons for the 'difficulty' John Wood finds is that the discourse usually operates separately from the theatrical effects, and the separation often involves vertiginous shifts of perspective. In moving from Shakespearian language to Stoppardian, or from the tragedy to the down-at-heel tragedians, or from Rosencrantz and Guildenstern as they present themselves at Elsinore to Rosencrantz and Guildenstern as they present themselves to us, we are not so much moving from one level to another as from one sphere to another which is either encasing it or encased within it. The conceit about the actors' lack of freedom within the deterministic script is the one still point within the shifting perspectives, but it might just as well not be still, because our own distance from it keeps changing as we are tossed cheerfully between macrocosm and microcosm. In the second act, for instance, Guildenstern appears to be discussing the possibility of improvising a way out of the script.

> Wheels have been set in motion, and they have their own pace, to which we are . . . condemned. Each move is dictated by the previous one—that is the meaning of order. If we start being arbitrary it'll just be a shambles: at least, let us hope so. Because if we happened, just happened to discover, or even suspect, that our spontaneity was part of their order, we'd know that we were lost.

[2] With A.C.H. Smith, see Bibliography.

These lines, as the audience knows, belong to Stoppard's script, and his spontaneity, at the moment of writing, was circumscribed by the impossibility of making Rosencrantz and Guildenstern do anything that could not be contained within the framework of Shakespeare's plot; but the image serves very well to reinforce the point that degrees of freedom cannot be measured as if the angle had nothing to do with perspective. The actor has to make decisions which to him seem very important, but they may make little difference to the audience. Everyone's life, like a tragedy written by God, moves relentlessly towards death and it is disconcerting to believe that it does not matter what we do with our circumscribed freedom of choice.

One of the main reasons Vladimir and Estragon need Godot is that it is intolerable for them to think that nobody is watching what they do[1]. Pozzo prolongs his conversation with them for the same reason. Stoppard translates the Beckettian need for a witness into a professional need for an audience. The tragedians are in constant danger of losing their identity, and they have to live through the actor's nightmare of losing the whole audience in mid-performance:

> You don't understand the humiliation of it—to be tricked out of the single assumption which makes our existence viable—that somebody is *watching* . . . There we were—demented children mincing about in clothes that no one ever wore, speaking as no man ever spoke, swearing love in wigs and rhymed couplets, killing each other with wooden swords, hollow protestations of faith hurled after empty promises of vengeance—and every gesture, every pose, vanishing into the thin unpopulated air.

Rosencrantz and Guildenstern can admit—as a hero never could—to the same need:

> The truth is, we value your company, for want of any other. We have been left so much to our own devices—after a while one welcomes the uncertainty of being left to other people's.

[1] See Ronald Hayman, *Samuel Beckett*.

Tom Stoppard

Like a Metaphysical poet, or a dog with a bone, Stoppard plays untiringly with his central conceit, never putting it down except to pick it up again, his teeth gripping it even more firmly. When Rosencrantz and Guildenstern hold a prose post-mortem on their last verse encounter with Hamlet, they are refreshingly like anyone trying to cheer himself up about a missed opportunity:

> GUIL: I think we can say we made some headway.
> ROS: You think so?
> GUIL: I think we can say that.
> ROS: I think we can say he made us look ridiculous.
> GUIL: We played it close to the chest of course.
> ROS *(derisively)*: 'Question and answer. Old ways are the best ways'! He was scoring off us all down the line.
> GUIL: He caught us on the wrong foot once or twice, perhaps, but I thought we gained some ground.
> ROS *(simply)*: He murdered us.
> GUIL: He might have had the edge.

Like Vladimir and Estragon they play defiant and dizzying games on the brink of acknowledging that they are puppets on the playwright's strings. Of course it's all less precarious than it looks because the strings will save them from falling. After keeping the dialogue going with two Jewish jokes in succession, Rosencrantz shouts into the wings:

> All right, we know you're in there! Come out talking! *(Pause)* We have no control. None at all . . . *(He paces)*

Desperate, he starts philosophizing about death. Unable to keep it up for long, he begins a joke about a Hindu, a Buddhist and a lion-tamer, only to break off:

> They're taking us for granted! Well, I won't stand for it! In future, notice will be taken. *(He wheels again to face into the wings)* Keep out, then! I forbid anyone to enter! *(No-one comes—Breathing heavily)* That's better . . .
> *(Immediately, behind him a grand procession enters, principally* CLAUDIUS, GERTRUDE, POLONIUS *and*

> OPHELIA. CLAUDIUS *takes* ROS*'s elbow as he passes and is*
> *immediately deep in conversation: the context is*
> *Shakespeare Act III, Scene i.* GUIL *still faces front as*
> CLAUDIUS, ROS, *etc, pass upstage and turn.)*
> GUIL: Death followed by eternity . . . the worst of both
> worlds. It is a terrible thought.

This bridges into Gertrude's conversation with Rosencrantz
about how Hamlet received them.

The movement between Shakespeare and Stoppard not only
raises questions of time and space, it also effectively creates a
confrontation between Elizabethan English and the English of
today. The transitions into the modern vernacular make the
twentieth century look lame, inarticulate and rather stupid in
comparison with the Renaissance. But the point is made in
comic terms, and never more amusingly than when Rosencrantz
and Guildenstern are allowed to watch Hamlet as he silently
contemplates suicide. The modern clichés make Rosencrantz
into a modern man:

> One might well . . . accost him . . . Yes, it definitely looks
> like a chance to me . . . Something on the lines of a direct
> informal approach . . . man to man . . . straight from the
> shoulder . . . Now look here, what's it all about . . . sort of
> thing. Yes. Yes, this looks like one to be grabbed with both
> hands, I should say . . . if I were asked.

Not that the vocabulary of the Elizabethan theatre—verbal or
silent—is always represented as superior. When Guildenstern
queries the purpose of the dumbshow, the Player answers: 'We
are tied down to a language which makes up in obscurity what it
lacks in style'. But generally it is the modern attitudes that show
up as vulgar or mindless:

> Well, really—I mean, people want to be *entertained*—they
> don't come expecting sordid and gratuitous filth.

While the poetic language of Shakespeare's central characters
makes them seem to be moving purposefully towards a tragic
climax, the prosaic dithering of Rosencrantz and Guildenstern

shows them to be circumambulating. Sometimes their theorizing is like that of the schoolboy who doesn't know the answer but thinks it safer to keep talking:

ROS *(thoughtfully)*: Madness, then.
GUIL: A matter of sore distraction.
ROS: Antic disposition.
GUIL: Which may or may not have been put on.
ROS: Which is another thing—he could have been a sane man pretending to be mad or a mad man pretending to be sane.
GUIL: Or a mad man who—didn't know he was mad but was pretending to be mad nevertheless.
ROS: That is to say, even madder than he didn't know he was.

While many plays appear to be vehicles for the jokes they contain, Stoppard's play is itself a gigantic joke which can breed and accommodate many smaller ones. Some of them are aimed at the medium, but the use of the medium is itself jokey. The third act opens in silence and in pitch darkness; the suggestion of nothingness, of death, is reinforced by the dialogue. Then suddenly the shipboard setting is being established ultra-theatrically. The sound which has been too soft to be identifiable turns out to be the sea. We hear voices shouting unmistakably nautical phrases at different distances and from different angles. Stoppard's stage direction asks for the point to be 'well made and more so', and when Hamlet lights a lantern, 'the stage lightens disproportionately'.

Sea travel is a theme which helps to develop the central idea: 'You don't have to worry about which way to go, or whether to go at all—the question doesn't arise'. You are moving even while keeping still; you are imprisoned but not in the same spot. We discover a small vestige of the *Lear* element from the original draft when Rosencrantz asks, 'Who is the English King?' and Guildenstern answers, 'That depends on when we get there'.

Again the theme of play-acting is introduced when Rosencrantz assumes the role of the King while Guildenstern plays both himself and Rosencrantz. We cut from one layer of unreality to another when they forget themselves sufficiently to break the seal on Claudius's letter. Finding that it asks for Hamlet to be killed, they have stumbled on an area of freedom and responsibility. Something, at last, depends on their choice. Should they go ahead or confide in Hamlet? The appearance of control over their three destinies is only illusory: he overhears their conversation and substitutes a letter asking for their deaths, but by then they have revealed that they would not have been strong enough to interfere with Claudius's plot:

> As Socrates so philosophically put it, since we don't know what death is, it is illogical to fear it. It might be . . . very nice. Certainly it is a release from the burden of life, and, for the godly, a haven and a reward. Or to look at it another way—we are little men, we don't know the ins and outs of the matter, there are wheels within wheels, etcetera—it would be presumptuous of us to interfere with the designs of fate or even of kings. All in all, I think we'd be well advised to leave well alone.

Before the end of the play they have discovered Hamlet's plot against them, but Stoppard is careful to be ambiguous about whether they do anything so definite as taking a decision not to go on living. Their death is represented theatrically by a conjuring trick: they disappear into the upstage darkness just before the dialogue switches back to the sequence from *Hamlet* which contains the announcement: 'Rosencrantz and Guildenstern are dead'.

Death is a recurrent theme in the third act, and the tragedians are well used in developing it. The indications of their presence on the boat leads pleasantly up to a characteristic pun. Music is heard, first from a pipe then from a drum, evidently inside the barrels. Finally the lid of the middle barrel pops open and the Player's head appears: 'Aha! All in the same boat, then!' Later, when Rosencrantz and Guildenstern discover the letter which Hamlet has forged, asking for their deaths, the tragedians are forming a menacing circle around them. Snatching a dagger from the Player's belt, Guildenstern talks angrily about the difference between the reality of death and the theatrical illusion of it:

> Even as you die you know that you will come back in a different hat. But no one gets up after *death*—there is no applause—there is only silence and some second-hand clothes, and that's—*death*—*(and he pushes the blade in up to the hilt. The* PLAYER *stands with huge, terrible eyes, clutches at the wound as the blade withdraws: he makes small weeping sounds and falls to his knees.)*

But this is only a theatrical death. We have already heard from the Player that when one of his actors was condemned to death and he arranged for the sentence to be carried out during a performance, the results were unconvincing.

In the first published edition of the play (May 1967) the action, like that of *Waiting for Godot*, is circular. Rosencrantz and Guildenstern may be dead but there is no shortage of attendant lords. Someone is shouting and banging on a shutter, indistinctly calling two names. But in rehearsals at the National Theatre, Stoppard cut this ending and in subsequent editions, as in performance, Shakespeare has the last word.

LORD MALQUIST AND MR MOON

Rosencrantz and Guildenstern Are Dead was premiered at Edinburgh during the same week that *Lord Malquist and Mr Moon* was published, so, as Stoppard has said[1], 'I was very light-hearted about the whole thing . . . there was no doubt in my mind whatsoever that the novel would make my reputation, and the play would be of little consequence either way'. It is not, in fact, unnatural that he should have had more confidence in the novel, which is the more elaborate of the two artefacts. Like the mid-sixties novels of Iris Murdoch and John Fowles, it is very much the work of a fabulator, to use Robert Scholes's word[2]. The fabulator is more concerned with intricacy and ingenuity of design than with reproducing a lifelike surface of appearances. Ideas and ideals become more important than objects or actions. Signalling the writer's awareness of his own limitations, comedy and irony license him to embark on absurdly ambitious schemes. Parody and self-parody have become inseparable.

'Nothing to be done,' says Estragon at the beginning of *Waiting for Godot*, meaning that it is no use trying to take his boots off; Vladimir replies as if they were discussing whether action can ever be worthwhile. 'Nothing,' says the ninth Earl of Malquist on the first page of the novel, 'is the history of the world viewed from a suitable distance.' He praises Louis XVI for writing 'Rien' in his private diary on the day the Bastille fell, and, within a page, the earl is arguing about boots. Wellington never had an original idea in his life, and the boots he wore should have been called Malquist boots.

In his useful *Encounter* article[3], Clive James suggests that Stoppard's universe is Einsteinian: he abandons fixed

---

[1] Interview with Janet Watts in *The Guardian*, see Bibliography.
[2] *The Fabulators*, Oxford University Press, 1967.
[3] November 1975. cf. Second Interview, page 141.

viewpoints. 'What looks odd when you stand over There is perfectly reasonable if you stand over Here . . .' he says, 'and now that you're Here, you ought to know that Here is on its way to somewhere else, just as There is, and always was.' We do not need to understand this conception of the time-space continuum: 'it exists to be ungraspable, its creator having discovered that no readily appreciable conceptual scheme can possibly be adequate to the complexity of experience.'

The novel resembles the plays in mingling abstruse argument with gaudy entertainment. Built into the plot is an infallible device for engendering suspense: Mr Moon, who is hired as Lord Malquist's Boswell, carries a bomb in his pocket. He also has a beautiful and magnetic wife. But these simple means of hooking the reader's interest are woven into an extremely complex design which involves literary parody. As in James Joyce's *Ulysses*, style is one of the main subjects, and amusing reverberations are set up between the style of the narrative, the life-style of the characters and their prose-style, both in conversation and in what they write. Lord Malquist is a Wildean creation: his epigrams, his clothes, his horse-drawn carriage and his outlook belong gloriously to the 1890s, and there is nothing sneaking about Stoppard's admiration for the panache to which privilege was conducive. He amuses himself and his readers by revelling in the style that Malquist incarnates, but he pits it against the austerities of the more democratic sixties.

Churchill is never named but his funeral procession winds its way through the narrative in almost the same way as *Hamlet* does through *Rosencrantz and Guildenstern*. Lord Malquist's comments are filtered to us through Moon's unreliable summary:

the extravagant mourning exacted from and imposed upon a sentimental people is the last flourish of an age whose criteria of greatness are no longer applicable . . . his was an age that saw history as a drama directed by great men. Accordingly he was celebrated as a man of action, a leader who raised involvement to the level of sacred duty, and he inspired his people to roll up their sleeves and take a militant part in the affairs of the world . . . the funeral might well mark a change in the heroic posture—to that of the Stylist, the spectator as hero, the man of inaction who would not dare roll up his sleeves for fear of creasing the cuffs.

Do we catch a faint echo of Prufrock's

I shall wear the bottoms of my trousers rolled.
Shall I part my hair behind? Do I dare to eat a peach?

There is some direct quotation from 'Prufrock' and a reference to *Hamlet*:

(That is not it at all,
that is not what I meant at all.
But when I've got it in a formulated phrase, when I've got it formulated, sprawling on a pin, when it is pinned and wriggling on the wall, then how should I begin . . .?)
And how should you presume?
(He's got me there, cold. How should I presume?)
All the same Moon knew that there was something rotten.

The funeral procession sometimes reminds us of the funeral procession that winds its way through James Joyce's *Ulysses*, but, as in *Travesties*, the voice we most often hear behind Stoppard's is that of Oscar Wilde:

He puffed delicately on Turkish tobacco papered in a heliotrope cylinder, and blew a perfumed wreath for the fading light.
'One must keep a dialogue of tension between the classes, otherwise how is one to distinguish between them? Socialists treat their servants with respect and then wonder why they vote Conservative.'
'I told you, dear boy. It is the duty of an artist to leave the world decorated by some trifling and quite useless ornament.'

Equally Wildean is the languid indifference to casualties. 'I am always bumping into people,' says Lord Malquist after a motor-cyclist has been killed by his coach.

The most extreme stylistic antithesis is provided by the cowboys. A confrontation between two characters can be a confrontation between two styles almost as contrasted as Elizabethan and modern English. Later, in writing dialogue for the cowboys, Stoppard will demonstrate his expertise as a mimic of theatrical and filmic clichés. He is also fluent in stage Irish and stage Jewish, the languages spoken by the donkey-rider who thinks he is the Risen Christ and the coloured coachman who works for Lord Malquist:

> 'Holy Mother, is it me papers ye're after, yer honour?'
> O'Hara jeered from his box: 'Papers-schmapers! A mile off I can smell a Yid!'
> 'O'Hara,' reproved the ninth earl, 'enough of this papist bigotry.'
> 'A Roman, are you?' asked the Risen Christ.
> 'I'm a Holy Catholic already!' shouted O'Hara. 'I should tell a lie?'

Almost as if Stoppard were throwing down a challenge to himself, the first chapter gives us flashes of events which seem not only improbable but disconnected: will he ever be able to make them cohere into a plausible story? Moon travelling in the earl's coach, inefficiently scribbling notes of his epigrammatic observations; Long John Slaughter moseying down a slope on his chestnut mare, a gun slung from his left hip; a lion watching a woman from behind a scrub of thorn; a dark man with thick matted curls riding side-saddle on a donkey; a slim girl with hair like spun gold ordering her French maid to tell Monsieur Jones that she is not at home; Moon conducting an interview with himself about why he carries a bomb. Can threads like these ever be interwoven convincingly? No one knows better than Stoppard that anything can be made convincing if it is made sufficiently stylish. The earl complains about other people's

> 'utter disregard for the common harmonies of life' . . . We live amidst absurdity, so close to it that it escapes our notice. But if the sky were turned into a great mirror and we caught ourselves in it unawares, we should not be able to look each

other in the face. He closed his eyes. 'Since we cannot hope for order let us withdraw with style from the chaos.'

Instead of withdrawing, Stoppard stylishly creates a chaos he can tidy up. We soon learn that Jane is Moon's wife, that the cowboys, who are not really cowboys, may have something to do with the promotion of Western Trail Pork 'n' Beans, that Malquist is liable to let his lion run loose in Hyde Park, and so on.

Nor are the narrative shifts mere devices for dizzying the reader. The vertigo of the short stories is being developed into something more meaningful—more communicable. Tormented by circumstantial but inconclusive evidence of Jane's infidelity, the desperate husband questions her.

> Every response gave Moon the feeling that reality was just outside his perception. If he made a certain move, changed the angle of his existence to the common ground, logic and absurdity would separate. As it was he couldn't pin them down.

All the nonsense in the novel makes sense if the absurdities are construed as problems that demand a solution. Stoppard, like Moon, is the struggling victim of a vision which presents all the phenomena of the present and the past as somehow interconnected:

> The rest of the world intruded itself in a cause-and-effect chain reaction that left him appalled at its endlessness; he experienced a vision of the billion connecting moments that lay behind and led to his simplest action, a vision of himself straightening his tie as the culminating act of a sequence that fled back into pre-history and began with the shift of a glacier.

This is one way the spectator can be a hero: to keep one's eyes unflinchingly open calls for almost heroic courage.

As in the best of Stoppard's plays, extreme seriousness co-exists happily with extreme frivolity. Even his private doubts about the value of his activity as a writer are fed back into the comic dialogue. Lord Malquist talks to Jane about Beau Brummell:

> 'You see, he understood that substance is ephemeral but style is eternal . . . which may not be a solution to the realities of life but it is a workable alternative.'
>
> Jane pressed against him as they wheeled back into Park Lane and headed south.
>
> Lord Malquist brooded on. 'As an attitude it is no more fallacious than our need to indentify all our ills with one man so that we may kill him and all our glory with another so that we may line the streets for him. What a nonsense it all is.'

Stoppard's artistic self-consciousness may have been highly developed before he began the novel, but it was apparently sharpened to an even finer point by the experience of writing it. Moon tells the coachman:

> 'I distrust attitudes . . . because they claim to have appropriated the whole truth and pose as absolutes. And I distrust the opposite attitude for the same reason. O'Hara . . .? You see, when someone disagrees with you on a moral point you assume that he is one step behind in his thinking, and he assumes that he has gone one step ahead. But I take both parts, O'Hara, leapfrogging myself along the great moral issues, refuting myself and rebutting the refutation towards a truth that must be a compound of two opposite half-truths. And you never reach it because there is always something more to say. But I can't ditch it, you see O'Hara.'

In manner this is remote from John Donne, but the Metaphysical poets also leapfrogged themselves along the great moral issues, defiantly holding to untenable premises, decorating absurdity with logic, transforming logic into drama. Stoppard shares their delight in teasing out ideas to such an extreme that they almost break, casually breathing an autobiographical cloud of cigarette smoke over the abstracting construction. He is bothered, for instance, as every writer is, by the knowledge that each sentence he puts down on paper represents a commitment which may be premature. Wouldn't it have been better to go on thinking about it until later in the evening? Moon is given a vision of himself 'as pure writer who after a lifetime of absolutely no output whatever, would prepare on his deathbed the single sentence that was the distillation of everything he had saved up, and die before he was able to utter it'.

Stoppard is also reminiscent of the Metaphysical poets in the pleasure he takes from wordplay and in the richness of the harvest he gathers from paradoxes. He even plays dialectical leapfrog with his deflations. Some of them become gestures that themselves ask to be deflated, and the narrative bloodstream is so infected with parody that the characters begin to feel guilty about literary echoes. *'Good grief,'* Moon reprimands himself, *'Wooster to the life.'* But he is talking to Birdboot, the butler, who is rather like a Wildean Jeeves. The parodies pile up against each other strongly enough for the resultant fiction to be appealingly original.

Peter Handke's title *The Ride across Lake Constance* recalls a legend about a horseman who crosses the frozen lake in safety, only to die of fright when he realizes that he might not have survived the ride. The existence of Stoppard's characters is equally precarious. 'My dear fellow,' says Lord Malquist, 'the whole secret of life is to carry on as if nothing has happened.' But he is better than Moon is at ignoring the symptoms of impending disaster: 'He felt the shell of human existence ballooning to a thinness that must give way at some point, and his whole nervous system was tensed for the apocalyptic moment.' The big power station is 'a constant threat to his peace of mind for it sat by the river, monstrous and insatiable, consuming something—coke or coal or oil or something—consuming it in unimaginable quantities, and the whole thing was at the mercy of a million variables any of which might fail in some way'.

Moon is 'afraid of all of the people some of the time and some of the people all of the time'. Malquist seems more confident. When asked what he stands for, he answers 'Style'. But his style is elegantly self-destructive; 'You know, Mr Moon, I could not bear to outlive my wealth, and since I am spending it more quickly than I am aging, I feel my whole life is a process of suicide.' But it is Moon who is spectacularly killed by the husband of the woman who was killed at the beginning of the novel, knocked down by the coach and pair. Moon is mistaken for Lord Malquist because he is riding in the coach. An accident, yes, but it fits beautifully into the design.

IF YOU'RE GLAD I'LL BE FRANK

When the BBC was planning *Strange Occupations,* a series of plays for Radio 3 about nonsensical and non-existent jobs, Stoppard was commissioned to provide a thirty-minute script. London telephones still had letters on the dials as well as numbers, and he was not alone in having his fancy caught by the recording of an unimpassioned female voice which would tell the time to everyone who dialled TIM. It is possible that there are still lonely men who already know what time it is when they dial 123, but now that the speaker cannot be associated with a human name, the illusion of contact has been diluted. No one would now think of paying tribute to her by writing a play about a bus driver who recognizes his wife's voice and comes to believe she is being kept in the GPO building against her will.

No other playwright, anyway, would have been prompted by her rhythmic time-announcements to compose verse in the style of T.S. Eliot. The TIM voice repeats itself exactly every twelve hours while almost repeating itself at each utterance.

> At the third stroke it will be eight fifty-nine and ten seconds . . . (PIP PIP PIP)
> . . . At the third stroke it will be eight fifty-nine and twenty seconds . . . (PIP PIP PIP)

So it sounds as though a movement forwards is being measured, though we know the recording is on a loop. An image of the human condition?

> Time present and time past
> Are both perhaps present in time future
> And time future contained in time past.
> If all time is eternally present
> All time is unredeemable.

Even if Stoppard was not directly influenced by *Four Quartets,* his verse bears a certain resemblance to Eliot's, both in its rhythms and in the attitudes it expresses:

> The point is beginning to be lost on me.
> Or rather it is becoming a different point.
> Or rather I am beginning to see through it.
> Because they think that time is something they invented,
> for their own convenience,
> and divided up into ticks and tocks
> and sixties and twelves and twenty fours . . .
> so that they'd know when the Olympic record has been broken
> and when to stop serving dinner in second-class hotels,
> when the season opens and the betting closes,
> when to retire;
> when to leave the station,
> renew their applications
> when their subscriptions have expired;
> when time has run out.

The latter part of this is oddly close to the choric uncles and aunts of *The Family Reunion,* though Stoppard had not read the play:

> We understand the ordinary business of living,
> We know how to work the machine,
> We can usually avoid accidents,
> We are insured against fire,
> Against larceny and illness,
> Against defective plumbing,
> But not against the act of God.

The idiom of Eliot's best work is so compellingly distinctive that, like his magnetized imitators, he almost seems to be parodying it when he is not writing so well.

Amusingly, Stoppard represents the Post Office as a hierarchy of complacent voices: Lord Coot, Sir John, Mr Courtenay-Smith and Mr Mortimer are as muddle-headed and as plummily self-important as the civil service bigwigs and the high-ranking military officers in radio comedy shows. Spoken contrapuntally against the background of her TIM announcements, which keep fading and returning, Gladys's private thoughts hit a serious level, especially when she reveals herself to be a victim of Stoppardian vertigo. She philosophizes about perspective:

> When you look down from a great height
> you become dizzy. Such depth, such distance,
> Such disappearing tininess so far away,
> rushing away,
> reducing the life-size to nothing—
> it upsets the scale you live by.

But, as always, there is rumbustious comedy to counterbalance the *Angst*. Frank keeps the passengers on his bus waiting while he gets off to dial TIM and talk to her with great urgency as she goes on telling him the time. In later sequences he parks his bus rebelliously in forbidden places, determined to break through to a confrontation with 'the top man in speaking clocks'. Like Gladys he is aimiably non-conformist: neither of them subscribes willingly to

> their alarm-setting, egg-timing, train-catching, coffee-breaking faith in an uncomprehended clockwork.

Bergson said that 'the comic is something mechanical encrusted on the living', and Stoppard has probably learned, like Ionesco, from Feydeau, whose plots ensnare human resistance into an accelerating clockwork mechanism. In the early Ionesco comedies, such as *Jacques or Obedience*, the hero rebels against the dehumanizing schedules of bourgeois conformism, and in *If You're Glad I'll Be Frank* the bus-driver and his wife try to snatch their moments of contact from the teeth of the all-devouring timetable, which is enforced by the overlords of the Post Office. These gentlemen may indulge privately in extra-curricular, extra-marital affairs, but they are all staunch and starchy upholders of the system who show no mercy in bringing the rebels back into line:

> 1ST LORD: Come on now, this isn't like you at all. Let's get things back on the rails, hm? Think of the public, Mrs Jenkins . . . Come on now . . . at the third stroke . . .

Tom Stoppard

GLADYS: At the third stroke . . .

1ST LORD: It will be five thirty-seven and forty seconds.

(PIP PIP PIP)

Carry on from there . . .

GLADYS: At the third stroke it will be five thirty-seven and fifty seconds . . .

A SEPARATE PEACE

Television is less conducive than radio to originality in writing because less depends on the words, and *A Separate Peace* is a less unconventional play than *If You're Glad I'll Be Frank*, though it is also about an unsuccessful attempt to escape from the normal social and commercial routines. John Brown, the middle-aged man who books himself into a nursing home, disconcerts the staff by not being ill. He can afford to pay for being nursed, so why should he *do* anything? As he later tells Maggie, the most attractive and most sympathetic girl on the staff, 'To stay in bed for tea is almost impossible in decent society, and not to get up at all would probably bring in the authorities. Even if you had the strength of character there's probably a point where it becomes certifiable'.

He causes no trouble in the nursing home and gives every sign of enjoying himself, but his presence embarrasses them, although there is no shortage of beds. There ought to be something wrong with him. Like Rosencrantz and Guildenstern he has no ambitions, and he is resigned to feeling bored. When the Matron says he mustn't lose interest in life, he tells her he was never very interested in the first place. Mainly to oblige her, he makes an attempt at basketwork, and when she suggests painting, he reveals that this is something he used to do. With the paints they provide he starts on a mural, a summer landscape.

> MAGGIE: It's summer outside. Isn't that good enough for you?
> BROWN *stares out of the window: gardens, flowers, trees, hills.*
> BROWN: I couldn't stay out there. You don't get the benefits.

As Maggie goes on trying to find out about his past, the audience shares her curiosity. After working at painting camouflage on tanks, he had four years of happiness as a

Tom Stoppard

prisoner of war, but Stoppard is canny enough to let him supply very little information. The closest point of resemblance to *If You're Glad I'll Be Frank* occurs when he talks of having wanted to be a monk:

> but they wouldn't have me because I didn't believe, didn't believe enough for their purposes. I asked them to let me stay without being a proper monk but they weren't having any of that.

Gladys had once wanted to be a nun:

> but they wouldn't have me because I didn't believe, I didn't believe *enough*, that is; most of it I believed all right, or was willing to believe, but not enough for their purposes . . . I asked her to stretch a point but she wasn't having any of it. I asked her to let me stay inside without being a proper nun, it made no difference to me, it was the serenity I was after, that and the clean linen, but she wasn't having any of that . . .

Clean linen is also one of the factors that attracts Brown to nursing homes.

Beckett's early fiction is full of heroes whose only ambition is to withdraw into isolation and inactivity. Belacqua, who appears in both *The Dream of Fair to Middling Women* (ca 1932) and *More Pricks than Kicks* (1934) was named after Dante's lutemaker who maintained: 'It is by sitting and resting that the soul grows wise'. Beckett's Belacqua wants 'to break not so much the flow of people and things to him as the ebb of him to people and things. It was his instinct to make himself captive . . .' In the novel *Murphy* (1938) the hero's favourite occupation is to lock the door of his room and tie himself naked to a rocking-chair.

Eventually John Brown is driven back into the world by the news that his sister Mabel and her husband are going to visit him. The relentless detective work of the doctor has led to the discovery that Brown has been in the nursing home before, when he was a child. Maggie has been helping the doctor by passing on all the information she gleaned. The final sequence is between her and Brown, but there is no sentimentality. She is on night duty in the hospital office when he appears, dressed, carrying his zipped bags. She ought not to let him go without waking the doctor, but she does.

ANOTHER MOON CALLED EARTH

'Plays,' says Stoppard[1], 'go off like fruit. They're organic things; they're not mineral. They change their composition in relation to the time they exist, or are seen to exist, and in relation to oneself; they start to decompose the moment the word is on the page.' Television plays decompose faster than stage plays, and retrospectively the main interest of *Another Moon Called Earth* is as a stepping-stone between *Lord Malquist* and *Jumpers*. In all three an attractive girl is confusing her husband between a rich mixture of evidence that suggests adultery and explanations that almost quell his suspicions. Is she as innocent as he hopes or as unscrupulous as he fears?

In neither play is there a character called Moon, but in both a landing on the moon replaces the funeral of the great statesman as a public event which changes the perspective—as if private actions will have to be judged differently from now on. Penelope is full of praise for the 'lunanaut':

> I tell you, he's smashed the mirror—finally, broken through—he has stood outside and seen us whole, all in one go, little. And suddenly everything we live by—our rules—our good, our evil—our ideas of love, duty—all the things we've counted on as being absolute truths—because we filled all existence—they're all suddenly exposed as nothing more than local customs—nothing more—Because he has seen the edges where we stop, and we never stopped anywhere before—
>
> BONE: Penelope—
>
> PENELOPE *(intensely)*: I'm telling you—when that thought drips through to the bottom, people won't just carry on.

After the attempts of Gladys and John Brown to withdraw

---

[1] Interview with Giles Gordon in *Transatlantic Review*. See Bibliography.

Another Moon Called Earth

from what Beckett calls the 'big blooming buzzing confusion of external reality', Stoppard makes Penelope take to her bed without any sign of being unhealthy. She's all right in bed, she says, ambiguously. Bone, whose sexual rapport with her has deteriorated into non-existence, is trying to write a book and has taken to sleeping on the divan in his study. She is unlike John Brown in not wanting to be bored, and as the play opens she is trying to lure Bone away from his work. Shouts of 'Fire!' and 'Murder' produce no reaction, but she succeeds with a vocal display of dwindling resistance to an imaginary rapist.

Marital bickering about unstated suspicions of infidelity gives way to arguments about the moon. Bone is unimpressed by the lunanaut: 'We all knew it was there. Nor did he have to navigate. He just—sat, really. And somebody had to be first. One thing leads to another; the last thing led to the moon'. Like Mr Moon in the novel, Bone is seriously (and comically) concerned about the causal interconnections between all the phenomena that have ever existed:

> You see, I'm not exactly a *historian*—the actual history has all been written up by other people—but I'm discovering the patterns—exposing the fallacy of chance—there are no impulsive acts—nothing random—everything is logical and connects into the grand design . . . I hadn't meant to do a history of the world, only of myself . . . but the thing kept spreading, making connections back, wider and deeper all the time, the real causes, and suddenly I knew that everything I did was the culminating act of a sequence going back to Babylon.

But Stoppard gives his audience no chance to be bored by philosophical speculation. Mystery is introduced with the disappearance of Pinkerton, Penelope's old nurse, who has gone on looking after her. Penelope claims to have given her the push, thrown her into the street, and when the old woman turns out to have been killed by a fall from the window, it seems that Penelope may be telling no more or less than the truth. The audience is teased with uncertainty, as it is during Penelope's explanations of the regular visits she has been receiving from

Tom Stoppard

Albert. The flowers he brings do not prove conclusively that he is not a doctor, and when Bone opens the bedroom door to find Albert kissing Penelope, it may be that all he has interrupted is a two-handed game of charades. Later, when he finds the drapes drawn around the four-poster bed, Albert's shoes are on the chair, together with his hat, cape and stick. There may be no good reason for a doctor to take his shoes off or get on to the bed before examining his patient, but why shouldn't he? Before he leaves, he grips Bone's shoulder sympathetically. Penelope, he announces gravely, is unable to leave her bed. She will never walk again. But when Bone goes into the bedroom, he finds her at the window, watching the lunanaut who is taking part in a parade to celebrate the moon landing:

> There goes god in his golden capsule. You'd think that he was sane, to look at him, but he doesn't smile because he has seen the whole thing for what it is—not the be all and end all any more, but just another moon called Earth.

ALBERT'S BRIDGE

By exploring the medium in his fifteen- and thirty-minute radio plays, Stoppard had taught himself a lot about the technique of writing for it, and his two sixty-minute plays *Albert's Bridge* and *Artist Descending a Staircase* are triumphs of expertise which challenge comparison with the best radio writing of Beckett and Pinter. Nearly all the motifs in *Albert's Bridge* are familiar from Stoppard's earlier work, but his development of them is original and impressive.

For Stoppard's purposes, a bridge which is high enough is like an accessible moon, offering a change of perspective. There was little of the Stoppardian vertigo in Penelope's attempts to empathize with the lunanaut's experience, but Albert, a university student, feels giddy with exhilaration when, to earn money during a vacation, he gets himself taken on as a painter working at the railway bridge above Clufton Bay:

> From the ground it looks just like a cat's cradle, from a distance you can take it all in, and then up there in the middle of it the thinnest threads are as thick as your body and you could play tennis on the main girders . . . It's absurd, really, being up there, looking down on the university lying under you like a couple of bricks, full of dots studying philosophy . . . I saw more up there in three weeks than those dots did in three years. I saw the context. It reduced philosophy and everything else. I got a perspective. Because that bridge was—separate—complete—removed, defined by principles of engineering which make it stop at a certain point, which compels a certain shape, certain joints—the whole thing utterly fixed by the rules that make it stay up.

In the final sentence the bridge becomes analogous to a work of art. At the same time Stoppard hits on the best dramatic image he has so far found for the impulse to reject the norms of bourgeois society: he makes Albert dedicate his life to bridge-painting. Without wasting space on maternal outrage or on satirizing the father, a self-made man who wants to give his son a job in Metal Alloys and Allied Metals, Stoppard finds a neat way of summarizing the rebellion against middle-class conventions while carrying the plot forward. Dismissing the pregnant maid with no sympathy and considerable self-righteousness, Albert's mother tells her, 'You'd better make sure that the young man does the right thing by you'. This is followed by a cut as abrupt, as telling and as funny as any in *The Dissolution of Dominic Boot*. We hear Kate saying, 'I never thought you'd do the right thing by me, Albert'.

The marriage, of course, is not a success. Albert is too much like Beckett's Murphy, who has been sleeping with a prostitute: 'The part of him that he hated craved for Celia, the part that he loved shrivelled up at the thought of her'. Albert is happy only on the bridge, and when Kate has nagged him into taking a Paris holiday with her, he is reluctant to come down from the Eiffel Tower:

> The pointlessness takes one's breath away—a tower connects nothing, it stands only so that one can go up and look down. Bridge-builders have none of this audacity, compromise themselves with function.

The marital relationship goes on deteriorating. Kate starts talking to herself out of loneliness, while he leaves home early and comes back late, preferring the solitude of work on the bridge.

But, like John Brown, he is not allowed to escape from society. His fate is in the hands of the Clufton Bay Bridge Sub-Committee, which is responsible for the upkeep of this symbol of the town's prosperity. While the provincial quartet of male voices may sound less educated than the one in *If You're Glad I'll Be Frank*, both are equally complacent and equally rigid in using schedules and budgets as a net: trapped employees are de-humanized by the loss of freedom. The least human of the four men is the City Engineer, Fitch, '*distinctive voice; clipped, confident; rimless spectacles*'. He uses mathematical arguments in favour of changing the present system by which four painters are employed. It takes them two years to paint the bridge, and this is the time the paint lasts, so the same men immediately begin all over again. With paint that lasted eight years, only one painter would have to be employed and the annual saving to the ratepayers would be £3,529.15.9. Albert, who likes working on his own, is given the job, but two years after the other three painters have been sacked, he has painted only a quarter of the bridge and the rest is looking very shabby.

Before the sub-committee has solved the problem, Albert's solitude has been disturbed by another refugee from local society. Fraser's language is 'poetic' but with an element of parody built into it.

> I came up because up was the only direction left. The rest has been filled up and is still filling. The city is a hold in which blind prisoners are packed wall to wall. Motor-cars nose each other down every street, and they are beginning to breed, spread, they press the people to the walls by their knees, pinning them by their knees, and there's no end of it, because if you stopped making them, thousands of people would be thrown out of work, and they'd have no money to spend, the shopkeepers would get caught up in it, and the farms and factories, and all the people dependent on them, with their children and all. There's too much of everything, but the space for it is constant. So the shell of human existence is filling out, expanding, and it's going to go bang.

He is suicidal because there is no design in the chain of accidents:

> there's nothing really holding it together. One is forced to recognize the arbitrariness of what we claim to be order. Somewhere there is a linchpin, which, when removed, will collapse the whole monkey-puzzle. And I'm not staying there till it happens.

He has come up to jump off the bridge but, seeing everything from above, he decides that 'the idea of society is just about tenable'. When he goes down, of course, it again becomes intolerable, so he comes back up, only to find once again that he has lost his urge to jump. 'My confidence is restored, by perspective.' The pattern would be capable of endless repetition were it not for the sub-committee's solution to the problem of deteriorating paintwork. 1,800 men are employed to paint the bridge. 'By nightfall the job will be done,' says Fitch. 'I have personally worked it out, and my department has taken care of the logistics.' Albert is up there arguing with Fraser when Stoppard produces an effect that would be impossible in any other medium. The same sound effect—marching feet and 'Colonel Bogey' being whistled—could be introduced in a stage or television play, but on the air the 1800 marchers are no less real—no less palpably present—than the two men who are describing what they see:

> Ten abreast—sixty deep—and another phalanx behind
> —and another—successive waves—
> *(The whistling is getting louder)*
> —so it has come to this.

Like Rosencrantz and Guildenstern, who are almost flattered by the tragedy of their deaths, never having believed themselves to be important enough, Albert is caught by surprise: 'Eighteen-hundred men—flung against me by a madman! Was I so important?' He knows that the basis of his existence is being destroyed; he does not yet know that his life is. The changing tone of the marching indicates that more and more of the men have left terra firma and started the ascent. Soon we hear the noise of rivets popping out of place. The tensed girders tremble under the weight of the workforce. Fraser's apocalyptic prophecies are being carried to dramatic fulfilment and Albert, his alter ego, dies with him as the bridge collapses.

THE REAL INSPECTOR HOUND

Of all the ingenious mechanisms in Stoppard's plots, the one in *The Real Inspector Hound* has the most tightly coiled mainspring. His first stage play since *Rosencrantz and Guildenstern*, it runs only long enough to be half of a double bill, and, like its predecessor, it could be described as a play outside a play. This time Stoppard is the author of both, which enables him to construct an even tighter interrelationship between the two levels of irreality. Once again he strips a theatrical situation of all possibilities of passing itself off as anything but a theatrical situation, but this time he does not represent it as an image of the human condition. He concentrates on contriving an intricate and richly comic pattern which will allow plentiful opportunities to his talent for parody.

That themes repeat themselves from play to play does not indicate a lack of inventiveness. On the contrary, only a writer of rare resourcefulness could possibly ring such effective changes on the same ideas. The two theatre critics watching the thriller are like Rosencrantz and Guildenstern in starting off as passive spectators[1], privileged to comment and mock from the sidelines but, progressively and relentlessly, they are drawn into an action which will eventually destroy them.

The corpse which is on stage from the outset creates a suspense which runs through the long silence while Moon studies his programme and through the long conversation with Birdboot, who is a first-stringer. Moon, a second-stringer, receives plenty of wry sympathy from Stoppard, who could remember what it felt like to seethe with impatient envy of the man who was blocking his progress up the journalistic ladder:

> Sometimes I dream of a revolution, a bloody *coup d'état* by
> the second rank—troupes of actors slaughtered by their

[1] They could almost equally well have been ordinary members of the audience.

understudies, magicians sawn in half by indefatigably
smiling glamour girls, cricket teams wiped out by marauding
bands of twelfth men—I dream of champions chopped
down by rabbit-punching sparring partners while eternal
bridesmaids turn and rape the bridegrooms over the sausage
rolls and parliamentary private secretaries plant bombs in
the Minister's Humber—comedians die on provincial stages,
robbed of their feeds by mutely triumphant stooges
—and—march—an army of assistants and deputies, the
seconds-in-command, the runners-up, the right-hand
men—storming the palace gates wherein the second son has
already mounted the throne having committed regicide with
a croquet-mallet—stand-ins of the world stand up!

Meanwhile Birdboot, who had dinner the previous evening
with the actress playing the ingénue, tries to persuade Moon to
give her a good notice. Cleverly interwoven with the
conversation of the two critics is the action of the thriller, a
hilariously enjoyable display of all the coincidences, clichés and
excesses that the genre invites. Mrs Drudge, the charwoman at
Muldoon Manor, just happens to turn on the radio at the
moment when programmes are interrupted for a police
announcement about an escaped madman who has last been
seen in the desolate marshes around Muldoon Manor. At the
same moment a man corresponding to the announcer's
description creeps on to the stage and creeps off again,
unnoticed by Mrs Drudge, who has also failed to notice the
corpse, though she is dusting her way towards it. Still without
seeing it, she moves the sofa, hiding it completely. From the
satirical niche he has built for himself Stoppard can toss out
grenades of devastating parody at both the thriller convention
and the language in which the critics approach it. In one silence,
Birdboot immodestly shows Moon colour transparencies of an
entire review he has written reproduced in neon outside the
Theatre Royal. In his efforts to be polite, Moon sounds as
though he is reviewing Birdboot's notice.

When Mrs Drudge answers the telephone, Stoppard lets her
feed information to the audience with appalling generosity:

The Real Inspector Hound

Hello, the drawing-room of Lady Muldoon's country residence one morning in early spring . . . this is all very mysterious and I'm sure it's leading up to something, I hope nothing is amiss for we, that is Lady Muldoon and her houseguests, are here cut off from the world, including Magnus, the wheelchair-ridden half-brother of her ladyship's husband Lord Albert Muldoon who ten years ago went out for a walk on the cliffs and was never seen again—and all alone, for they had no children.

In her ensuing conversation with the mysterious stranger, who reappears, suavely giving his name as Simon Gascoyne, both of them pour out prodigious quantities of the facts that help to establish the preliminaries of a murder plot.

MRS DRUDGE: I pop in on my bicycle when the weather allows to help in the running of charming though somewhat isolated Muldoon Manor. Judging by the time you did well to get here before high water cut us off for all practical purposes from the outside world.

SIMON: I took the short cut over the cliffs and followed one of the old smugglers' paths through the treacherous swamps that surround this strangely inaccessible house.

In the next pause Moon speculates whether Puckeridge, the third string, is waiting for his death with the same impatience that he is waiting for Higgs's.

Felicity, the ingénue, who enters in her tennis clothes, reveals herself as being very much more enamoured of Simon than he is of her, but when Lady Muldoon makes her appearance, he seems passionately interested, as do Birdboot from his seat and Magnus from his wheelchair. Birdboot decides that her performance is 'one of the summits in the range of contemporary theatre'. Moon, who thinks he is talking about the younger actress, suggests that 'trim-buttocked' is the right word.

Inspector Hound's entrance is nicely prepared. Another radio announcement informs us that police in the vicinity of Muldoon Manor are being hampered by the deadly swamps and the fog.

Tom Stoppard

Almost immediately a 'mournful baying hooting' is heard in the distance and then repeated, nearer. Inspector Hound makes his appearance carrying a foghorn and wearing swamp boots—inflatable pontoons with flat bottoms about two feet in width.

> HOUND: I don't know—but I have reason to believe that one of you is the real McCoy!
> FELICITY: The real what?
> HOUND: William Herbert McCoy who as a young man, meeting the madman in the street and being solicited for sixpence for a cup of tea, replied, 'Why don't you do a decent day's work, you shifty old bag of horse manure', in Canada all those many years ago and went on to make his fortune. *(He starts to pace intensely.)* The madman was a mere boy at the time but he never forgot that moment, and thenceforth carried in his heart the promise of revenge! *(At which point he finds himself standing on top of the corpse. He looks down carefully.)* Is there anything you have forgotten to tell me?

The obvious suspect is Simon, who does not reappear until the stage is empty. Birdboot is experienced enough to know that a murder is about to be committed. A shot rings out. Simon falls dead. Hound runs on to crouch by the body. Who killed Simon Gascoyne?

With great satirical sophistication, Stoppard pokes fun not only at thrillers and critics but at himself. 'It is at this point,' declares Birdboot, 'that the play for me comes alive. The groundwork has been well and truly laid, and the author has taken the trouble to learn from the masters of the genre. He has created a real situation, and few will doubt his ability to resolve it with a startling dénouement.' Turning on the 'public' voice that both characters use for their 'sustained pronouncements' of critical opinion, Moon adds: 'the author has given us—yes, I will go so far—he has given us the human condition'. Stoppard even contrives a side-swipe at the critics who have tried to analyse the influences on his work. 'I will not attempt,' declaims Moon, 'to refrain from invoking the names of Kafka,

Sartre, Shakespeare, St Paul, Beckett, Birkett, Pinero, Pirandello, Dante and Dorothy L. Sayers.

Immediately after this the two critics become directly implicated in the action of the thriller. I do not know whether the American humorist Robert Benchley was the first member of an audience to answer a telephone that was ringing on stage; I assume that *The Real Inspector Hound* was the first play to show a member of the audience succumbing to the temptation. Benchley, apparently, announced to the audience: 'It's for me'. When Moon answers he tells Birdboot, 'It's for you'. His wife, Myrtle, is on the line and soon he is plunged into the same desperate self-justification he has been attempting in his conversations with Moon. If he takes actresses out to dinner it is 'simply by way of keeping *au fait* with the world of the paint and the motley'. (Stoppard's males are always less adept than his females at making excuses.) Birdboot has rashly crossed the frontier into that world, and when Felicity makes another entrance through the French windows in tennis clothes, it is to him she addresses the same flirtatious dialogue she used with Simon. But Birdboot has come to the same conclusion as Simon: that Cynthia Muldoon is more desirable, so the sequence runs parallel to the earlier one until Felicity flounces out with the same red herring of a threat: 'I'll kill you for this, Simon Gascoyne!'

Birdboot's next dialogue is with Mrs Drudge, and again a combination of ingenuity and serendipity enables Stoppard to contrive a parallel to her scene with Simon after the rejected Felicity's first flouncing exit. In his conversation with her, Birdboot's lines did not exactly echo Simon's; in his conversation with Mrs Drudge, they do:

MRS DRUDGE: I have come to set up the card table, sir.

BIRDBOOT *(wildly)*: I can't stay for a game of *cards*!

MRS DRUDGE: Oh, Lady Muldoon *will* be disappointed.

BIRDBOOT: You mean . . . you mean, she wants to meet me . . . ?

MRS DRUDGE: Oh yes, sir, I just told her and it put her in quite a tizzy.

Tom Stoppard

From his seat in the stalls, Moon tries to rescue his colleague, but when Cynthia enters, it becomes hopeless:

> CYNTHIA: Don't say anything for a moment—just hold me.

Birdboot, who had suspected her of kissing onstage with her mouth open, is delighted to find that he was right. In the ensuing game of cards with Magnus and Felicity, the language becomes surrealistically confused:

> CYNTHIA: I think I'll overbid the spade convention with two no-trumps and King's gambit offered there—*(discards)* and West's dummy split double to Queen's Bishop four there!
> MAGNUS *(as he plays cards)*: Faites vos jeux. Rien ne va plus. Rouge et noir. Zero.
> CYNTHIA: Simon?
> BIRDBOOT *(triumphant leaping to his feet)*: And I call your bluff!
> CYNTHIA *(imperturbably)*: I meld.

In the interval, when Birdboot is left alone on stage, Moon accuses him of turning the play into a farce. It is then that Birdboot recognizes the corpse. Who would want to kill Higgs? Moon, who has most to gain, is insisting that he didn't do it, when another shot rings out and Birdboot falls dead. As Moon rushes onto the stage, the two critics' seats are immediately occupied by Simon and Hound, who become vengeful champions of all the actors and characters in thrillers that have suffered at the hands of critics: 'One has only to compare this ragbag with the masters of the genre to see that here we have a trifle that is not my cup of tea at all'.

Magnus now addresses Moon as Inspector, and he accepts the role, rashly eager to solve the mystery of his colleague's murder. The characters are unimpressed by his rather journalistic attempt at reconstructing past events, and Moon is himself coming under suspicion until Magnus pulls off his moustache to proclaim himself the real Inspector Hound. Recognizing him as Puckeridge, the third-stringer, Moon realizes too late that he is in danger. He backs away. 'Stop in the name of the law!' warns

Hound alias Magnus alias Puckeridge, and when Moon turns to run for it, he is shot. Puckeridge has not merely climbed two rungs of the journalistic ladder, he now reveals his fourth identity which wins him the desirable Cynthia:

> Yes!—it is me, Albert!—who lost his memory and joined the force, rising by merit to the rank of Inspector, his past blotted out—until fate cast him back into the home he left behind, back to the beautiful woman he had brought here as his girlish bride.

Casually, almost unintentionally, Stoppard is making the point that the contemporary whodunnit has its roots in melodrama.

Like *Rosencrantz and Guildenstern, The Real Inspector Hound* gained enormously from rewriting spread over a long period. Stoppard was still living in Bristol when he wrote the first draft and he hit on the name Moon as a result of seeing the film *The Left-Handed Gun*. A character called Moon is killed by the hero. One sequence (possibly derived from the chapter titled 'Moony' in D.H. Lawrence's *Women in Love*) shows the men shooting at a reflection of the moon in a horse-trough. An early draft of *The Real Inspector Hound* contained a sequence in which somebody shouted out the name of one of the critics rather in the same way that Paul Newman, in the film, shouted out the name Moon.

The recurrence of the names Boot and Birdboot in Stoppard's work has roots in his period as a journalist, when he sometimes wrote under a pseudonym:

> I've always been attracted to the incompetence of William Boot in Evelyn Waugh's *Scoop*—he was a journalist who brought a kind of innocent incompetence and contempt to what he was doing. I'd always thought that William Boot would be quite a good pseudonym for a journalist, so I used it, and got quite fond of Boot as a name.[1]

It is easy to read too much significance into the repetition of names, but, as Stoppard says, 'Moon is a person to whom things

---

[1]   Interview in *Theatre Quarterly*, see Bibliography.

happen. Boot is rather more aggressive'. He has also said (to me):

> In some limited sense I write about the same character a lot, and I think I've got a small, unimportant neatness complex. Occam's razor. Keep the names down. Don't proliferate nomenclature unnecessarily. So I use them whenever they might help. But it's pure coincidence that I've written about the moon in *Jumpers*. The only vaguely interesting aspect of the whole matter is that I find it a serious block to be arbitrary about naming characters. There is a curious sense of their having to be correctly named.

NEUTRAL GROUND

It was characteristic of Stoppard, with his anti-autobiographical bias, never to use the line 'England isn't my country, you know' until he came to write an ephemeral television thriller. When Granada commissioned a script from him for a series based on classical myths, he reworked the story of Philoctetes into a suspenseful plot centring on a Slav, whose code name used to be Philo when he worked for the British. Suspecting him of being a double agent, they finally left him marooned on neutral territory.

The parallel with Philoctetes is cleverly contrived. After he had been bitten by a snake, the stench of his wound was so offensive that Odysseus and the Greeks, who were on their way to Troy, abandoned him on an island. But he was still in possession of the infallible bow and arrows that Heracles had given him. Without these Troy would never be conquered. So the Greeks had to come back. The plays that Aeschylus and Euripedes wrote on the subject survive only in fragments, but Sophocles's version is still intact, and in this Odysseus is shrewdly opportunistic and cowardly, ignominiously retreating when Philoctetes threatens to shoot an arrow. Neoptolemus, Achilles's son, is unlike Odysseus in feeling compassion for Philoctetes and in being honest with him.

Stoppard follows Sophocles in leaving his Odysseus character, Otis, in the background, while the Neoptolemus figure, Charles Acheson, works on Philo. Odysseus makes insufficient allowance for the integrity of Neoptolemus, who sabotages his leader's plot. It is thanks to the intervention of the God Heracles that Philoctetes accompanies the Greeks to Troy. In Stoppard's play a series of expertly phased revelations show that Acheson, though more honest than an agent can afford to be, is less honest than he seems, bitterly though he chafes against the feelingless calculation which is characteristic of Otis and of the Secret Service.

Tom Stoppard

The action is set in a country adjacent to Austria where for five years Philo has been doing almost nothing, but, unlike John Brown, he is not happy to do nothing. He wants to go home, although his country has disappeared even from the maps. 'It's just another Soviet state, the same colour as all the rest, without even the thinnest line to show where it used to start; the politicians have been sanctified by the map makers.' This is why he wanted to work for the British.

Otis, a high-ranking British Intelligence man, now wants him back, and Acheson, who succeeds in winning Philo's confidence, is briefed to get him on the train that will carry him into the hands of the British. The climaxes are carefully prepared and effectively detonated—especially the last one when Philo, having failed to persuade Acheson to stay on neutral ground, saves him from unpleasant repercussions by jumping onto the moving train at the last minute. The clash of personal and political considerations is a recurrent subject in Stoppard's plays, and it was characteristic that he could introduce several of the serious themes that involve him underneath the surface of a thoroughly workmanlike thriller.

TEETH

It might be interesting to have a series of television plays based on fantasies of revenge that jealous husbands have entertained. Dentistry is a profession that can form an ideal basis for sadistic daydreams of this sort. In reality it must happen very seldom that a vengeful dentist gets his wife's lover into the chair, but television is a good medium for exploring what he could do if he did. The camera can move in close on eyes dilated with fear about what is happening inside the mouth; our own anxieties about teeth and sexual attractiveness make us more vulnerable in the privacy of our home than we would be in a cinema; sandwiched between newsreels and studio discussions, the fantasy takes on a dangerous aura of reality.

Tom Stoppard's thirty-minute script puts the dentist, Harry, in a very strong position. His wife, Prudence, has been seduced by George, the husband of his receptionist, Mary. Some of the *doubles entendres* are not up to the level of Stoppard's best ('You won't find anything wrong with my choppers!' 'In flashing form, are you?') But he is always very good at dealing with excuses and alibis. He makes the most of such ambiguities as 'I can spot the signs, you know', which could refer either to decay or duplicity. Tortured both by the sophisticated dental equipment and by Harry's sophisticated technique of withholding information about how much he knows, George is driven into some impetuous improvisations, but the situation becomes most amusing when his capacity for invention is being most severely tested. How will he explain the fact that Prudence came home wearing Mary's shoes?

The situation moves onto the edge of farce when Stoppard introduces a liquid which Harry says is good for the gums but liable to stain the teeth green. George is warned not to move his head, and when it does go on one of his teeth, Harry's comment is 'Lucky it's that one. I'm afraid he won't be needing it anyway'.

Tom Stoppard

Not content with reducing George's sex appeal by removing one of his middle teeth, Harry takes advantage of Mary's responsiveness. After flirting with her ostentatiously and adjusting the ear-rings he has given her, he disappears with her behind the dentist's chair. We see George's eyes in close-up as he tries to turn his head. When Mary reappears, her nurse's cap is askew. Harry then asks permission to keep her late, giving an obviously specious reason for needing her.

THE ENGAGEMENT

The Dissolution of Dominic Boot packed a great deal of narrative information into fifteen minutes. It was inevitable that when the radio script was expanded to fill fifty minutes of television, some of the subtlety would be lost.

The Engagement starts the story before Dominic goes out to lunch. We see him in his office with a sheaf of legal papers on his desk. Mistaking a telephonist's voice for his fiancée's, he tells her that he has been thinking about her all night. His confrontations with the disapproving Mr Cartwright have comic potential of a more familiar kind, and the introduction of ten beautiful office girls is extravagant in a way that tends towards destroying the attractive simplicity of the original script. We now meet Vivian in the jeweller's shop, where she bullies Dominic into buying a more expensive engagement ring than he wanted to give her, and it is this which leaves him short of cash. He eats only an omelette for lunch, and the fact of his having several bank accounts is established by making him produce three cheque books from his pocket in the Wimpy Bar. After he has dropped Vivian off at the library, we see him driving to Coutts Bank in the Strand and, when he fails to extricate enough cash to pay the taxi, to the Co-op Bank in Notting Hill. Here the manager pursues him into the taxi, which increases the 'Extras' on the fare from 6d to 1/-.

A spectacular sequence is introduced at the office, where Mr Cartwright looks out of the window at a crowd which has collected in the street, apparently to look at him. In fact it is looking at Dominic, who has climbed out of a window in order to climb in through the window of Cartwright's office. Two policemen and a priest come up in the lift. It sounds as though the cash problem is solved when the beautiful girls say that they have collected money to give him an engagement present, but they have bought a hideous ornament, a half-naked negress, which he clutches through the remainder of the action.

81

As before, he goes home to raid his gas meter and tries unsuccessfully to borrow from his mother. A new episode involves a thief with a stocking over his head who mistakes the taxi for his getaway car and a policeman who uses the taxi to pursue the thief, but this merely increases the amount on the meter. In another new sequence Dominic tacks himself on to a troupe of buskers and collects half a crown from Lemon, who is smoking a cigar in his taxi and tosses the coin out of the window without looking up from his newspaper.

There is a new sequence in a hospital where Dominic tries to borrow money from a doctor he knows and ends up by giving three transfusions of blood in order to collect ten shillings for each. In his debilitated state he meets Vivian, and from his quarrel with her we cut, as before, to the sequence in which he bargains with Lemon about a price for the engagement ring. He goes on as before, to sell him everything he owns. We end, as before, with a sequence in which he turns up at the office in pyjamas and a raincoat. Again it is raining and again the girl who tries to be kind calls a taxi, saying he can drop her off.

Much of the new detail is effective enough in itself and Stoppard's inventiveness has adapted itself well to the visual medium, but the result would have been better if he had been able to fulfil his original intention of stretching the radio play into thirty minutes of television. But the only company the director could interest in the script was NBC, who insisted on fifty minutes.

AFTER MAGRITTE

Magritte's 1934 painting *The Human Condition* shows a canvas on an artist's easel standing in front of a window. The three legs of the easel, the studded side of the canvas and the clip which holds it in place are painted with meticulous realism, as is the landscape on the canvas and the landscape we see through the window. About half the total area occupied by the window is blocked by the canvas, but we see exactly what we would see if the canvas were not there, or if it were transparent, except that our view through the window is interrupted by the clip, the studded edge and the tops of the three legs. But why is the painting called *The Human Condition*? Since we are looking at a painting, the 'real' landscape outside the window is only an image. The landscape on the canvas is an image of an image. But when we look directly at a real landscape, do we ever possess more than an image of it?

Magritte's painting and the point it makes may have been in Stoppard's mind when he wrote about the would-be recluse who enjoyed painting a summer landscape on the wall of his room in the nursing home more than he would have enjoyed being in the open air. Magritte often used the painting-within-the-painting to make statements about perception which are also, indirectly, statements about the human condition. This is probably one of the reasons he fascinates Stoppard, whose use of the play-within-the-play is comparable.

In a series of eighteen illustrated pronouncements about the relationship between objects, images and names, Magritte wrote: 'Sometimes the name of an object takes the place of an image . . . An object never fulfils the same function as its name or image'. He illustrates this with a drawing of a horse, a painting of a horse and a man saying the word 'horse'. He did not paint particularly well and, deprived of their titles, many of his works would be devoid of interest: Magritte intended the titles to 'accompany' the pictures 'in the way that names

Tom Stoppard

correspond to objects, without either illustrating or explaining them'. In one of his best known paintings the caption 'This is not a pipe' accompanies the image of a pipe: the relationship between caption and image is neither one of illustration nor of explanation. Nor is the caption inaccurate: an image of a pipe is not a pipe.[1]

In spite of Jarry's plays and Artaud's polemics, surrealism exerted little influence on mainstream theatre before Ionesco, whose most surreal effects always come as the climax of an elaborate development. At the end of *The Chairs*, for instance, the stage is full of empty chairs and littered with streamers and confetti which have been thrown over the invisible Emperor. The Old Man and the Old Woman have jumped out of the window. The last character to leave the stage was the Orator, who is dumb. Suddenly we hear sounds coming from nowhere or from the invisible crowd—laughter, whispering, coughing. This creates a theatrical image that would have appealed to André Breton, who said in 1948: 'For me the only real evidence is a result of the spontaneous, extra-lucid and defiant relationship suddenly sensed between two things which common sense would never bring together'. Lautréamont (1847-70) had created an image which became a prototype for the surrealists: 'As beautiful as the chance meeting on a dissecting table of a sewing machine and an umbrella'.

In the tableau that opens *After Magritte* an old lady in a bathing cap is lying on an ironing board with a white bath towel over her body and a black bowler hat on her stomach. Standing on a chair is a half-clothed man wearing evening-dress trousers under thigh-length green rubber fishing waders. He is blowing upwards into the metal lampshade which is on a pulley, counter-weighted by a basket overflowing with apples, oranges, bananas, pineapple and grapes. An attractive woman in her thirties is on her hands and knees, wearing a full-length ballgown. The furniture, including a settee, a television set and a gramophone with an old-fashioned horn is all stacked against the street door. Looking in through the window is a helmeted

---

[1]   cf. Stoppard's remark in the interview, page 3.

Stephen Moore (left) as Harris, Malcolm Ingram (policeman) as Holmes, Josephine Tewson (on ironing-board) as the mother-in-law, and Prunella Scales (on floor) as Thelma, in *After Magritte* at the Ambience Theatre Club.

police constable. The initial impact is very much like that of a surrealist painting, but instead of orbiting away from everyday reality as Ionesco does, Stoppard moves gradually towards it as the mysteries are explained. We are reminded of *Lord Malquist*.

The man, Harris, is trying to cool the bulb, which is too hot to handle. The furniture has been piled up to clear space for some last-minute ballroom dancing before a professional appearance. He is bare to the waist because his dress shirt has to be ironed.

Tom Stoppard

He has been wearing waders to replace a bulb in the bathroom while the bath was full. The wife, Thelma, is on her hands and knees because she is looking for her shoes. The mother-in-law has been lying on the ironing-board for a massage. The policeman is there because the Harrises' car has been traced as having been parked in Ponsonby Place near the Victoria Palace at 2.25 this afternoon. According to the hypothesis of Inspector Foot of the Yard, a one-legged nigger minstrel, using his crutch as a weapon, stole money from the box-office: Harris may have been an accomplice.

Tom Stoppard sometimes tells a story about a rich friend who had peacocks in his garden. They are valuable birds and, one day, while he was shaving, he glanced out of the window to see one of them jumping over the garden wall. Still in his dressing gown and with lather covering one side of his face, he rushed out in pursuit of the bird, which had crossed to the other side of the street before he caught it. With it tucked firmly under his arm, he had to wait for several cars to pass before he could cross back over the road. What interests Stoppard is the afterlife of the image in the minds of people who all tend to re-edit visual memories until they make sense. How do you make sense of a man standing on the pavement in a dressing gown with shaving cream on one side of his face and a peacock under his arm?

After Magritte is structured around the creation and solution of two mysteries: the visual riddle presented by the opening stage picture and the other visual riddle which is presented not in visual but in verbal terms. Thelma thinks that a man they passed in the car this afternoon was a one-legged footballer clutching a football. Harris insists that he was wearing not a football shirt but pyjamas, that he was carrying a turtle or a tortoise, that he had a white beard and must have been blind because he had a white stick. The Mother-in-law's memory of him is different: 'He was playing hopscotch on the corner, a man in the loose-fitting gabardine of a convicted felon. He carried a handbag under one arm, and with the other he waved at me with a cricket bat.' It turns out that Inspector Foot, who happens to live in Ponsonby Place, left his car on a yellow line overnight. He slept late, saw a car pulling away from a parking space while he was in the middle of shaving, grabbed his wife's handbag and, to keep off the rain, her white parasol, which he failed to open, and in his haste to put on his pyjamas, put both feet into the same leg. No robbery has been committed: the surmise was based on the report of an elderly lady, a neighbour in Ponsonby Place, who telephoned the police about the broken crutch and coins spilled on the pavement.

Behind the play Magrittean principles can be discerned: that similarity does not prove identity; that there is no logic of causality to map the relations between things, images and names.

To round the play off, Stoppard works his way towards a final tableau which is hardly less bizarre than the opening. Inspector Foot takes the bulb out of the socket to prove his contention that a one-legged man cannot hold his balance in the dark. When the light comes on again, Mother is playing the tuba, standing on one foot on a chair which is on the table. Inspector Foot, with one foot bare, is eating a banana and wearing sunglasses. Harris is wearing Thelma's ballgown and a cushion cover over his head. Thelma is in her underwear, crawling around the table. Together with everything else, Stoppard's brief script comfortably accommodates justifications for this final tableau.

WHERE ARE THEY NOW?

This is a thirty-five-minute radio play which shuttles between an Old Boys' reunion dinner in 1969 and a school dinner during the last year of the war. In the twenty-four year gap the masters have changed relatively little while the boys have grown up. The climacteric event at the reunion occurs when Gale, instead of standing up in silent memory of a teacher who recently died, stays in his seat and talks:

> We walked into French like condemned men. We were too afraid to *learn*. All our energy went into ingratiating ourselves and deflecting his sadism on to our friends. We brought him lumps of French to propitiate him until the bell went, and some of it stuck, that's all—right, Brindley? . . . What a *stupid* man! I think we would have liked French. It is not, after all, a complex language.

Hearing that the man who used to be one of his two best friends is now sending his son to the school, Gale launches into a scathing attack on the system:

> God, I wish there was a way to let small boys know that it doesn't really matter. I wish I could give them the scorn to ride them out—those momentous trivialities and tiny desolations. I suppose it's not very important, but at least we would have been happier children, and childhood is Last Chance Gulch for happiness. After that, you know too much. I remember once—I was seven, my first term at prep school—I remember walking down one of the corridors, trailing my finger along a raised edge along the wall, and I was suddenly totally happy, not elated or particularly pleased, or anything like that—I mean I experienced happiness as a state of being: everywhere I looked, in my mind, *nothing was wrong*. You never get that back when you grow up; it's a condition of maturity that almost *everything* is wrong, *all the time*, and happiness is a

borrowed word for something else—a passing change of emphasis.

Emotional intensity of this kind, unrelieved by comedy, occurs very seldom in Stoppard's work; the rhythms and some of the phrasing are oddly reminiscent of John Whiting (the other playwright with whom Peter Wood found a great affinity). But the construction is characteristically Stoppardian. Ever since *Rosencrantz and Guildenstern* he seems to have enjoyed paying the heavy taxes he has levied on his own resourcefulness by setting himself the task of finding new ways to move between two layers of action. *Neutral Ground* had been the only earlier script in which the lapse of time had created the distance between the two layers. In treating the subject of school it is obviously advantageous to flash backwards and forwards in a zigzag pattern: we focus not only on the differences between the intimidated schoolboys and the men they become, but also on the sameness, which raises the question of how much the school has conditioned their development, or even arrested it. Revealing vestiges of schoolboy slang remain in their adult vocabulary. But Stoppard is more interested in contrast than causality; though the play incidentally demonstrates that adult jokiness has roots in schoolboy attempts to evade embarrassment. The main weakness in the play is that the flashbacks do so little towards testing the validity of Gale's criticisms. The comedy, which is prominent and successful, has almost nothing to do with them.

Wartime austerity is evoked by a sequence in which the boys deliberately confuse rock salmon with dogfish; the comedy of schoolmasterish facetiousness is explored (and implicitly criticized) when we hear that Mr Dobson was resorting to sarcasm twenty-four years ago in defence of his sadistic colleague:

> Do stop crying and take your plate away. You really shouldn't get into such a state over Mr Jenkins. He no doubt has a thankless task trying to educate you in a subject that will prove invaluable to you in later life should you join the Foreign Legion, which most of you will probably have to.

Tom Stoppard

The joke Stoppard builds up most elaborately is about a seventy-year-old man with the same name—Jenkins. None of his memories coincide with those of Dobson, who thinks he is an impostor, while he thinks Dobson's mind has gone. There is a place-card with the name Jenkins on it and it is not until the end of the evening, when the school song is sung, that the old man gives himself away as having been at another school which is holding its Old Boys' reunion dinner in a room downstairs. The place-card has been put there by mistake for the dead French master.

Stoppard manages to say quite a lot through names. Gale is named after John Gale, the author of *Clean Young Englishman*, whom Stoppard imagined as having the same kind of neurotic intensity. Nicknames, too, are important in the play. Dobson used to be called Dobbin, while the three friends, Gale, Brindley and Marks were known as Groucho, Chico and Harpo. Retrospectively, the main importance of *Where Are They Now?* is as a first draft for *Artist Descending a Staircase*, which also flashes backwards and forwards in time to tell the story of a triangular male friendship that survived from school into old age.

The conformist pressures of society are represented in *Where Are They Now?* not by a quartet of male voices but by the whole evocation of the public school system and by the representative voice of the headmaster. As in *If You're Glad I'll Be Frank*, Stoppard likes to get two speeches going simultaneously and to fade the more repetitive or the more predictable down to inaudibility. While the headmaster is making a speech about where the most successful old boys are now, Dobson asks Gale why he came. The Headmaster's voice continues under Gale's reply:

GALE: I wanted to see if I'd got him right—if he had any other existence which might explain him . . . As it is, he'll have to go to my grave as I remember him. Still, perhaps he remembered me as a minor bully and a prig, which I was.

JENKINS: Some of us have happier memories.

GALE: Oh yes, the snows of yesteryear . . . *(Agonized)* Where were they *then*? Oh, where the Fat Owl of the Remove, where the incorruptible Steerforth? Where the Harrow match and your best friend's beribboned sister? Whither Mr Chips. Oh no, it's farewell to the radiators and the punishable whisper, cheerio to the uncomprehending trudge through *Macbeth* and sunbeams defined by chalkdust, the sense of loss in the fruitcake sent from home, the counted days, the hollow fear of inconsiderable matters, the hand raised in bluff—*Sir, sir, me sir!*

The near-lyrical nostalgia assorts rather oddly with the Eliot pastiche. Certainly there is a degree of irony and the self-conscious literariness is intended to be self-deflating, but the resultant attitude is less well defined than usual in Stoppard. Extreme seriousness and outrageous comedy have not quite joined hands.

DOGG'S OUR PET

The title is an anagram of Dogg's Troupe, Professor Dogg being a pseudonym of Ed Berman, the American director of Inter-Action, the community arts organization which had presented lunchtime performances of *After Magritte*. Dogg's Troupe is one of his theatre groups and he describes it as 'primarily interested in developing new forms of participatory theatre, and exploring environmental and street theatre for mixed audiences of children and adults'.

Though *Dogg's Our Pet* can be enjoyed without any knowledge of modern philosophy or modern painting, the principle behind it is both Wittgensteinian and Magrittean. As Stoppard explains in the Preface, a man engaged in building a platform out of planks, blocks, bricks, cubes and slabs of wood may be shouting out the words 'Plank', 'Block', 'Brick', 'Cube' and 'Slab'. If another man is throwing him bits of wood in different sizes and shapes, an observer would assume that the sizes and shapes correspond to what he shouts.

But this is not the only possible interpretation. Suppose, for example, the second man knows in advance which pieces Charlie needs, and in what order. In such a case there would be no need for Charlie to 'name' the pieces he wants, but only to indicate when he is ready for the next one. So the calls might translate thus:

Plank = Here!
Slab = Ready!
Block = Next!
Brick = the thrower's name.
Cube = thank-you!

This creates an alternative language, and the scene works equally well whether both men are using it, or one man is using it while the other uses normal English.

And if life for Charlie and Brick consisted only of building platforms in this manner there would be no reason for either of them ever to discover that they were each using a language which was not understood by the other. But this happy state of affairs would end when a third person begins to use the language in a way which is puzzling to either Charlie or Brick.

It would be hard to dismiss the idea as uninteresting but easy to make the mistake of dismissing it as untheatrical. Few other playwrights would have been able to develop it in a way which raises so many laughs and leaves an audience feeling so satisfied. The mathematician, the engineer, the entertainer and the surrealist in Stoppard have collaborated very happily and, as usual, the audience is given the feeling of entering fully into the fun he has had at his desk. It is a more abstract play than *After Magritte*, with less delineation of a situation and less narrative, but it uses combinations of words and actions to create rhythms which arouse audience expectations. As in music, these are sometimes satisfied, sometimes satisfyingly frustrated.

The first word spoken is 'Plank', at which a plank is thrown from offstage into Charlie's waiting hands. But when he repeats the word, a football is thrown on. Two schoolboys appear, throwing the ball around, interrupting the sequence by which planks, slabs and blocks are thrown to Charlie, mimicking his habit of spitting on his hands in readiness to catch the next bit of wood, and shouting out words themselves, also in mimickry. The word 'Plank' is shouted seven times, 'Slab' five times and 'Block' three times. Throughout the first half of the script, every word of dialogue is monosyllabic. The next word—'Dogg'—is a warning that the Headmaster is coming. He wears a mortarboard and a black gown. He is handing out small flags on sticks to the front row of the audience and to the three characters on stage as he counts, 'Sun, dock, trog, slack, pan, sock, slight, bright, nun, tuns, what, dunce'. To dispel any doubt that what he means is 1, 2, 3, 4 etc, his last figure, 'dunce', is challenged. This prompts a recount.

The word 'Block' (meaning 'Next') is used four times by Dogg as he distributes flowers. It is only when Charlie uses the word in sarcastic mimickry that a wooden block is thrown on from the wings. He then shouts 'Brick' four times, receiving four bricks from his invisible mate. When Dogg enters shouting 'Brick', a fifth brick is thrown. Charlie is surprised but manages to catch it, while the two schoolboys reply by showing Dogg where Brick is standing. Dogg goes offstage to give him a flag and a flower. The next time Charlie shouts 'Brick', a cube is thrown on instead. He needs a brick because he is now constructing steps to the platform. When he repeats the order, another cube is thrown. He sees that two cubes = one brick, so he is able to complete the fourth step. Stoppard has carefully calculated how the platform is to be constructed, and he is helpfully precise in his specifications of relative sizes. A brick is twice as long as it is wide and it is equal in cross-section to a block. A slab is equal in length to six blocks. A slab is not as long as a plank and it is square in cross-section.

The Headmaster's organizing talent is now used to speed up the action's clockwork mechanism. Confiscating the ball, he arranges the two schoolboys and Charlie in a straight line. Cubes are handed rapidly down the line and positioned on top of the bricks. When Charlie says 'Cube' he means 'Cube'; when the others say it, they mean 'Thank you'. They each say the word seven times as seven cubes are rapidly added to the structure, but the eighth, ninth and tenth times Charlies shouts 'Cube' he receives a slab.

When he stops work to switch his radio on, we hear football results translated into the language Dogg was using when he counted up to 'dunce' (= 12). 'Quite' means nil; 'Clock' means city and 'Foglamp' means United. But though the inflections will sound familiar, the meaning will be indecipherable in performance when the announcer says: 'Dogtrot quite, Flange dock; Cabrank dock, Blanket Clock quite; Tube Clock dock, Handbag dock; Haddock Clock quite, Haddock Foglamp trog; Wonder quite, Picknicking pan'.

Stoppard has contrived that there are by now three slabs and six blocks on stage which have not gone into building the platform. Indecipherable signs have been scrawled all over all six sides of all nine pieces, but when the schoolboys build them up into a wall, the scrawls are made to compose into the words

DOGG
POUT
THERE
ENDS

Meanwhile Dogg has unfurled a ribbon in the school colours all across the stage, but when Charlie smiles at Dogg, Dogg knocks him against the wall, disintegrating the cryptic message.

After Dogg has unrolled a red carpet, the two boys rebuild the wall, with the blocks in different positions. A new message is displayed, equally meaningless. Again Dogg knocks the wall over by knocking Charlie against it. The next message is

DONT
UPSET
DOGG
HERE

At the same time as the message is acquiring meaning, the actions we have been watching begin to make sense. As in *After Magritte*, the development of the action gives us a means of interpreting them. The flags, the flowers, the platform, the ribbon and the red carpet all belong to the preparations for a launching ceremony. The play has been built around the occasion for which it was commissioned, the opening of Inter-Action's Almost Free Theatre in Rupert Street. A well-dressed Lady (who may be either the Queen or the Chairman's wife) makes her appearance. She walks along the red carpet, followed by a smirking Dogg, who carries a pair of golden scissors on a cushion. The Lady's majestic tone and formal delivery are surrealistically at odds with her words:

> Scabs, slobs, black yobs, yids, spicks, wops . . . Sad fact, brats pule puke crap-pot stink, spit; grow up dunces crooks; rank socks dank snotrags, conkers, ticks; crib books, cock snooks, block bogs, jack off, catch pox, pick spots, scabs, padlocks, seek kicks kinks, slack: nick swag, swig coke, bank kick-backs; frankly cant stick kids.

Tom Stoppard

When she cuts through the ribbon she says: 'Sod the pudding club!' The school song is sung, a posy is presented, the Lady leaves and, after confronting Dogg, Charlie voluntarily hurls himself at the wall—a variant on the old music-hall routine by which the Moon or Laurel character is suddenly one step ahead of the Boot or Hardy character, who has been meting out all the punishment.

Beginning to dismantle the construction, one of the boys tosses a cube towards the wings with a shout of 'Brick!' 'Cube,' corrects Charlie, who now climbs up to make a speech:

> Three points only while I have the platform. Firstly, just because it's been opened, there's no need to run amuk kicking footballs through windows and writing on the walls. It's me who's got to keep this place looking new so let's start by leaving it as we find it. Secondly, I can take a joke as well as any man, but I've noticed a lot of language about the place and if there's one thing I can't stand it's language. I forget what the third point is.

He then reassembles the wall to make the message read

DOGGS
TROUPE
THE
END

JUMPERS

Only a passionate lover of wordplay would have written the two lines in *Rosencrantz and Guildenstern* which was to become the germ of *Jumpers*[1]:

—Shouldn't we be doing something constructive?
—What did you have in mind? . . . A short, blunt human pyramid . . . ?

Starting from a narrow base, Stoppard uses puns to cantilever out into the metaphysical void. In becoming more intricate, his architecture annexes more space. *Jumpers* is, by any standards, an extremely big play. Wanting to write about a moral philosopher and seeing the verbal connection between mental acrobatics and the pyramid of acrobats—unless they are acrobats it will be too short and blunt—Stoppard seems to have found that the multiple meanings of the word *jump* helped him to evolve his blueprint.

The audience's first encounter with the word comes near the beginning, when Archie's voice announces 'And now!—ladies and gentlemen!—the INCREDIBLE—RADICAL!—LIBERAL!!—JUMPERS!!' and four of them come on from either side of the stage, jumping, tumbling and somersaulting. Already coupled with the name of a political party, the word soon acquires an overtone of expediency. Dotty—the counterpart of Penelope in *Another Moon Called Earth*—drunkenly orders them to jump when she says jump; the one character in the play who will not 'jump along with the rest' is George, who is stubbornly,unfashionably, a deist in the materialistic university which serves as a microcosm for the new society. He is temperamentally incapable of 'jumping through the Vice-Chancellor's hoop'. In the second act we find out that the surname of Sir Archibald, the Vice-Chancellor, is Jumper, and

---

[1]   cf. Interview, page 4.

when he refuses to let George succeed the murdered McFee into the Chair of Logic, he says he needs 'someone with a bit of bounce'. By the end of the play we have been persuaded to associate the word *jump* with Kierkegaard's leap to faith. George says:

> The fact that I cut a ludicrous figure in the academic world is largely due to my aptitude for traducing a complex and logical thesis to a mysticism of staggering banality. McFee never made that mistake, never put himself at risk by finding mystery in the clockwork, never looked for trouble or over his shoulder, and I'm sorry he's gone but what can be his complaint? McFee jumped, and left nothing behind but a vacancy.

All these proliferations of *jump* are new, but much of the basic material is developed from *Lord Malquist and Mr Moon* and *Another Moon Called Earth*, with some drawn from *Albert's Bridge* and some from *After Magritte*. If it is not already clear that I approve of Stoppard's self-plagiarism, let me make it clear now. The advantage of returning to areas that have already been explored is that one has learnt which routes lead most directly to the points of interest. Even in territory which is not autobiographical, there is always an excitement in exploring. Strongly self-disciplined though he is, Stoppard is liable to become over-excited on his first expedition: the idea is then over-elaborated. In the television play *Another Moon Called Earth*, as in the novel *Lord Malquist and Mr Moon,* charades are used as a camouflage by the wife who seems to be deceiving her husband. The sequences are highly entertaining, but the charades of *Jumpers* make their points more economically and more casually. The argument between George and Dotty is not interrupted when she takes the goldfish into the bathroom, returning with its empty bowl over her head as she imitates the leaden-footed gait of a moonwalker. Her pretence of picking up a small coin gives George the clue he needs and he interpolates the answer—'The Moon and Sixpence'—into his monologue without even pausing.

Like the millionaire who put only coin telephones at the

disposal of his house guests, Stoppard's plays grow richer by economizing and economize more as they grow richer. It is characteristic of him not to waste the goldfish. An hour later, George returns from the bathroom, full of righteous indignation, the fish dead in his hands: 'You murderous *bitch*! . . . You might have put some water in the bath!' The phrase has two layers of meaning because it seems she may have murdered Professor McFee, the empiricist who has been shot out of the acrobatic pyramid. And if Stoppard refuses to characterize Dotty consistently as a musical-comedy actress, one reason is that it would be uneconomical not to arm her with the wit she needs for intellectual combat with George.

DOTTY: Don't you dare splash me with your sentimental rhetoric! It's a bloody goldfish! Do you think every sole meunière comes to you untouched by suffering?

GEORGE: The monk who won't walk in the garden for fear of treading on an ant does not have to be a vegetarian . . . There is an irrational difference which has a rational value.

DOTTY: Brilliant! You must publish your findings in some suitable place like the *Good Food Guide*.

GEORGE: No doubt your rebuttal would look well in the *Meccano Magazine*.

DOTTY: You bloody humbug!—the last of the metaphysical egocentrics! You're probably still shaking from the four-hundred-year-old news that the sun doesn't go round *you*!

In developing his architectonic virtuosity Stoppard has refined his capacity for accommodating both halves of a contradiction. Part of the appeal that puns have for him may lie in the means they provide of coupling the unrelated meanings of a single sound, but few of his conceits remain merely verbal. There are puns in George's monologues when he reminisces about the punctuality of his late friend Bertrand Russell, and theology and ethics are described as two subjects without an object. But the pun becomes more like a jump-cut in a film when George, having ignored Dotty's gambit (modelled on Penelope's) of shouting, 'Murder—Rape—Wolves!' prematurely shoots the arrow from his bow when she shouts 'Fire!' There are also the visual puns of her charades: lying nude and apparently lifeless on the bed, she is *The Naked and the Dead*; a vertical view of her naked back later prompts the guess '*Lulu*'s back!—in town'.

One of Stoppard's greatest talents is for profiting from experience. Each new play has been an exercise, both in the sense of testing how far he can go and in the sense of giving himself practice that develops his muscles for future performance. Coming after he had taught himself to write for radio, the achievement of *Dogg's Our Pet* gave him new insight into the possibilities of making words and actions mutually independent. To employ both in the same statement may be extravagant; the playwright may be able to economize not only by giving dialogue a double meaning but by saying something separate and perhaps contradictory with the accompanying action.

Not that Stoppard is ungenerous or incapable of extravagance when it serves a purpose. In contrast to the calculated monotony of the coin-tossing sequence at the beginning of *Rosencrantz and Guildenstern*, the opening of *Jumpers* is spectacularly spendthrift. Dotty is given an upbeat introduction as if she is about to sing, and there is the immediate anti-climax of her failure. There is the striptease performed by the poker-faced Secretary on a swing hanging from a chandelier. There is the vaudeville-type comedy of the porter's appearance with a tray of drinks, wandering innocently towards the point at which he will be knocked over. There is the circus-type performance of the Jumpers, tumbling and somersaulting. There is the first rumble of marital conflict when George protests at the noise, and the first indication that Dotty in on the verge of a mental breakdown—both implicitly promising dramatic tension. Then there is the murder. With the acrobats standing on each other's shoulders in three-two-one formation, a shot rings out. A man in the bottom row falls dead. Dotty walks through the gap in the pyramid. The dying man pulls himself up against her legs, shedding blood on her billowy white dress. The pyramid collapses. It is almost as if Stoppard were taking excessive precautions against the possibility that his play would be condemned as wordy and boring.

In spite of everything, the anonymous critic in the *Times Literary Supplement*[1] wrote: 'Stoppard's "theatrical" antics are seen to be decoration for a drama which is essentially static. *Jumpers* is textbook stuff which reduces both the actors and the audience to the level of readers, a dead-end for the drama'. I believe, on the contrary, that his antics are pointing a way forwards.

Nothing is harder for the serious critic to forgive than jokiness, but Stoppard's jokiness should be viewed against the perspective provided by James Joyce, Samuel Beckett and Modernist painting. For Joyce the pun was sometimes a self-indulgence, sometimes a means of bridging between conscious and unconscious memories. In *Ulysses*, as in Beckett's earlier novels, the most serious philosophical and theological problems are broached with a fruitful mixture of self-conscious literariness, literary self-consciousness and exuberant flippancy. Joyce is reported to have said of *Ulysses*: 'On the honour of a gentleman there is not a serious line in it'. But no one today would argue that the incessant joking makes the book unimportant, though it could be objected (as it could with Stoppard's plays) that the ingenuity of the pattern-making claims an unfair share of the creative energy.

Stoppard could hardly be accused (as Joyce has been, by Harry Levin) of equating language with experience, but they are both open to attack from the argument that structural intricacy camouflages a philosophical void. One of the main filters through which Joyce's influence passes into Stoppard's work is Beckett's fiction, especially *Murphy*, his first full-length novel. Murphy's mind

> pictured itself as a large hollow sphere hermetically closed to the universe without . . . He neither thought a kick because he felt one nor felt a kick because he thought one . . . Perhaps there was, outside space and time, a non-mental non-physical Kick from all eternity, dimly revealed to

[1] 29 December 1972

Tom Stoppard

Murphy in its correlated modes of consciousness and extension, the kick *in intellectu* and the kick *in re*. But where then was the supreme Caress?

Stoppard's recurrent Moon character is 'more kicked against than kicking'.

Stephen's stream of consciousness in *Ulysses* ripples along with the same mixture of wry hopelessness and triumphant word-spinning erudition in the involuntary attempt to explain the inexplicable relationship between the individual consciousness and the constants of the cosmos and of human reproduction:

Wombed in sin darkness I was too, made not begotten. By them, the man with my voice and my eyes and a ghost-woman with ashes on her breath. They clasped and sundered, did the coupler's will. From before the ages He willed me and now may not will me away or ever. A *lex eterna* stays about him. Is that then the divine substance wherein Father and Son are consubstantial? Where is poor dear Arius to try conclusions? Warring his life long on the contransmagnificandjewbangstantiality.   Illstarred heresiarch. In a Greek watercloset he breathed his last: euthanasia.

While Rosencrantz's and Guildenstern's comic attempts to solve the cosmic riddles may be more reminiscent of Vladimir's and Estragon's, George Moore's derive more directly from the Joycean voice of Stephen. Stoppard has succeeded magnificently in canalizing the stream of highly educated consciousness into hilarious theatricality:

To begin at the beginning: is God? *(Pause)* I prefer to put the question in this form because to ask, 'Does God exist?' appears to presuppose the existence of a God who may not, and I do not propose this late evening to follow my friend Russell, this evening to follow my late friend Russell, to follow my good friend the late Lord Russell, *(He ponders a moment)* To ask, 'Is God?' appears to presuppose a Being who perhaps isn't . . . and thus is open to the same objection as the question, 'Does God exist?' . . . but until the difficulty is pointed out it does not have the propensity to confuse language with meaning and to conjure up a God who may have any number of predicates including omniscience, perfection and four-wheel-drive but not, as it happens, existence. This confusion, which indicates only that language is an approximation of meaning and not a logical symbolism for it, began with Plato and was not ended by Bertrand Russell's theory that existence could only be asserted of descriptions and not of individuals, but I do not propose this evening to follow into the Theory of Descriptions my very old friend—now dead, of course—ach!—to follow into the Theory of Descriptions, the late Lord Russell—!

(He continues smoothly, improvising off-script)

if I may so refer to an old friend for whom punctuality was no less a predicate than existence, and a good deal more so, he would have had us believe, though why we should believe that existence could be asserted of the author of 'Principia Mathematica' but not of Bertrand Russell, he never had time, despite his punctuality, not to mention his existence, to explain, very good, keep to the point, to begin at the beginning: *is God?*

(To SECRETARY*)* Leave a space.

The puns are more functional than Joyce's because they contribute more to the structure. They also buoy the performance of the speech on waves of laughter.

George's interest in the Greek philosopher Zeno may derive from Beckett's. Zeno used the example of a heap of millet to argue that movements in space and time are discontinuous with reality, the essence of reality being infinity. If you pour half a sack of millet into a heap, and then add half of what's left in the sack, and then go on adding half of what's left in the sack, you will never empty it, because you are moving in space and time. In infinity, all the grains would pass from the sack to the heap. In *Endgame* the implication for Hamm is that however long you go on living, the minutes never add up to a life because the end is always ahead of you. Zeno also argued that an arrow in flight i. always at rest since, at any given moment, it is where it is. Hi ambition was to prove that there could be no such thing a change: there are things but no changes. The rival argument—championed by both Heraclitus and Henri Bergson—is tha there are changes but no things. The chapter on Bergson ir Bertrand Russell's *History of Western Philosophy* introduces S Sebastian to illustrate the difference between the two attitudes According to the 'static' school he is killed by the arrow according to the 'dynamic' school by its flight. Stoppard let: George suggest that the saint died of fright.

The confusion of the argument about Achilles and the tortoise with the fable about the tortoise and the hare is quite fruitful Together with George's illustrative bow and arrow, a tortoise and a hare are introduced into the action. Like most elements ir a Stoppardian structure, they are used in several ways: both become prominent in the multi-layered theatrical jokes. It is the

Michael Hordern as George in the National Theatre production of *Jumpers*.

death of the tortoise which provides one of the main comic climaxes. Distressed at his long-delayed discovery that he has killed the hare by shooting the arrow, George steps backwards onto the tortoise. The disappearance of the hare, Thumper, has created a minor mystery that has run through the plot, interwoven with the mystery of McFee's murder by some fine comedy of misunderstanding. When, in George's hearing, Archie praises the casserole he is sharing with Dotty, she replies, 'It's not casseroled. It's jugged.' After the affair of the goldfish, there is only one conclusion George can draw, and when the porter, Crouch, comes in, he is talking about McFee while George is talking about Thumper:

GEORGE: Who killed him?
CROUCH: Well, I wouldn't like to say for certain . . . I mean, I heard a bang, and when I looked, there he was crawling on the floor . . .
  (GEORGE *winces*)
  . . . and there was Miss Moore . . . well—
GEORGE: Do you realize she's in there now, *eating* him?
CROUCH (*pause*): You mean—*raw*?
GEORGE (*crossly*): No, of course not!—*cooked*—with gravy and mashed potatoes.
CROUCH (*pause*): I thought she was on the mend, sir.
GEORGE: Do you think I'm being too sentimental about the whole thing?
CROUCH (*firmly*): I do not, sir.

Apart from her premature retirement, Dotty gives no sign of wanting to withdraw from contact with humanity, but her instability is a continuation from that of characters in Stoppard's earlier plays. In his most solipsistic moments, the Albert of *Albert's Bridge* was in the habit of crooning to himself and muddling one lyric with another:

'cos there'll be pennies fall on Alabama
and you'll drown in foggy London town
the sun was shi-ning . . . on my Yiddisher Mama.

Dotty's confusions are more pointedly limited to moon songs,

105

and, like Penelope in *Another Moon Called Earth,* she lost her perspective when the astronauts landed on the moon. Penelope retired to her bed; Dotty retired.

> They thought it was overwork or alcohol, but it was just those little grey men in goldfish bowls, clumping about in their lead boots on the television news; it was very interesting, but it certainly spoiled that Juney old moon; and much else besides.

Her main disorientation speech draws on Penelope's, but it is stronger and more resonant, partly because Dotty has been more fully characterized, and partly because her cosmic disenchantment is complementary to George's stubborn theism:

> Not only are we no longer the still centre of God's universe, we're not even uniquely graced by his footprint in man's image . . . Man is on the Moon, his feet on solid ground, and he has seen us whole, all in one go, *little—local* . . . and all our absolutes, the thou-shalts and the thou-shalt-nots that seemed to be the very condition of our existence, how did they look to two moonmen with a single neck to save between them? Like the local customs of another place. When that thought drips through to the bottom, people won't just carry on. There is going to be such . . . breakage, such gnashing of unclean meats, such coveting of neighbours' oxen and knowing of neighbours' wives, such dishonourings of mothers and fathers, and bowings and scrapings to images graven and incarnate, such killing of goldfish and maybe more—*(Looks up, tear-stained)* Because the truths that have been taken on trust, they've never had edges before, there was no vantage point to stand on and see where they stopped. *(And weeps.)*

After George has expounded McFee's philosophy that there is no absolute or metaphysical sense in which telling the truth is 'good' and casual murder is 'bad', we hear Dotty trying to put his murder into perspective: 'It's not as though the alternative were immortality.'

Meanwhile the old Stoppardian theme of the credulous

husband is being given a new dimension of serious interest by the comic investigation of how it is possible for us to believe anything:

> How does one know what it is one believes when it's so difficult to know what it is one knows? I don't claim to *know* that God exists, I only claim that he does without my knowing it, and while I claim as much I do not claim to know as much; indeed I cannot know and God knows I cannot.

Later he says 'There are many things I know which are not verifiable but nobody can tell me I don't know them'.

Alongside this good-humoured philosophical sabotage, Stoppard is sharpening his parody of the thriller to the point where there almost seems to be a metaphysical resonance even in the characterization of a policeman as corruptible and seducible. If everyone can be persuaded to distort or overlook the facts about past events, do they still have any solid existence or any meaning? Inspector Bones is an autograph-collecting Dotty-fan with one foot in *After Magritte* and the other in *The Real Inspector Hound*. Her romantic reception of him is like an episode from the play-within-the-play:

> *In front of the Bedroom door, he briefly smooths his hair, brushes his lapels with his hands, brings out the gramophone record (which has a picture of* DOTTY *on it), and knocks on the Bedroom door, a mere tap, and enters the Bedroom. The light is romantic: pink curtains have been drawn across the french window and there is a rosy hue to the lighting.* DOTTY, *gowned, coiffed, stunning, rises to face the Inspector. Music is heard . . . romantic Mozartian trumpets, triumphant.* DOTTY *and* BONES *face each other, frozen like lovers in a dream.* BONES *raises his head slightly, and the trumpets are succeeded by a loud animal bray, a mating call.* DOTTY, *her arms out towards him, breathes, 'Inspector . . .' like a verbal caress. From* BONES*'s lifeless fingers, the vase drops. There is a noise such as would have been made had he dropped it down a long flight of stone stairs.*

Tom Stoppard

Just as words can be made to register separately from the accompanying actions, actions can be made to register separately from the accompanying sound effects, creating a mystery which will be resolved by a subsequent development. George has simultaneously been rehearsing an illustration he has prepared for his lecture. The tape-recording contrasts beautiful Mozartian trumpet music with the trumpeting of an elephant and the noise made by a trumpet falling downstairs. Stoppard's joke is essentially theatrical: its effect depends on the progressive reaction of an audience. There is also some self-indulgent pattern-making in the play, like the allusion to *After Magritte* when Inspector Bones makes his first entrance: George is holding a tortoise in one hand and his face is covered in shaving foam. But most reprises of earlier themes are more rewarding for the audience. The point Stoppard made about unicorns in *Rosencrantz and Guildenstern* is developed into something much more interesting during one of Dotty's speeches about astronauts:

> When they first landed, it was as though I'd seen a unicorn on the television news . . . It was very interesting, of course. But it certainly spoiled unicorns. *(Pause)* I tried to explain it to the analyst . . . I should never have mentioned unicorns to a Freudian.

It would be a mistake to end this chapter without stressing the pathos of the human situation in *Jumpers*. It is an oceanic play with a glistening surface and chillingly profound undercurrents, but bobbing stubbornly about, like survivors clinging to the driftwood of a shipwrecked culture, are Dotty and George. Stoppard gives us a lively and sympathetic impression of their personal needs. When they reach out towards each other, they fail to make contact; when they reach out elsewhere, they are pathetic, especially George, with his old-fashioned scruples about ethics and language. Like a more articulate and logical Lucky, he struggles for semantic clarity as he tries to reason his way backwards towards a First Cause, but he is deriving his values and his words from a system which is disintegrating. Traditional ethics cannot survive in a universe where quarrelsome jumpers can land on the moon, churches are converted to gymnasiums, an agnostic agriculturalist is appointed by the government as Archbishop of Canterbury and the police can be persuaded to connive at murder.

ARTIST DESCENDING A STAIRCASE

If Stoppard could not have written *Jumpers* without having written *Another Moon Called Earth*, *After Magritte*, *The Real Inspector Hound* and *Lord Malquist and Mr Moon*, *Travesties* could not have been written without the experience of *Artist Descending a Staircase*, which depended on the experience of *Where Are They Now?* Stoppard has a genius for refining his own architectural ideas. The new play is not restricted to shuttling between the present and one period of the past: it tells the story of a lifelong friendship between three artists by situating its eleven sequences in strategically patterned positions. The first and last sequences are set in the present; the second and tenth a few hours previously; the third and ninth a week earlier; the fourth and eighth in 1922; the fifth and seventh in 1920; the sixth in 1914. So the chronological structure is like a V with its lowest point in the first year of the First World War.

Like most of Stoppard's plays, *Artist Descending a Staircase* could have been written only by a man who enjoys arguing with himself and crystallizing the contradictions into characters. The mainspring of both this play and *Travesties* is the debate about art which has been going on for years inside Stoppard's brain. Is art useless? Should it have a social purpose? Anyway, what is it? Does the artist need a special skill, or can anyone produce anything he pleases and then see whether other people are gullible enough to accept it as art? The three artists argue incessantly about theories of art and about their own practice. Beauchamp makes avant-garde tapes of unmelodious *musique concrète*, insisting that they could appeal to an audience of millions if only the BBC would champion them. Donner insists that the artist is

> someone who is gifted in some way which enables him to do something more or less well which can only be done badly or not at all by someone who is not thus gifted. To speak of an

art which requires no gift is a contradiction employed by people like yourself who have an artistic bent but no particular skill.

After experiments in creating edible art, he has returned to traditional values, while Beauchamp has been recording *musique concrète,* and Martello fabricating visual metaphors, with corn for hair and pearls for teeth.

Around the arguments, Stoppard has constructed a work of art which is itself an argument in defence of the art that assumes a discontinuity between the world outside the mind and the world inside. As in *Jumpers*, the plot pivots around the mystery of a death which is explained only at the last minute. Once again Stoppard is using the mystery not merely to generate theatrical suspense but to show that experience is inseparable from interpretation and that interpretations are liable to be grotesquely inaccurate. Developing the idea he used in Dotty's meeting with Inspector Bones, Stoppard starts the play with an ambiguous tape-recording, which will be used by Martello and Beauchamp in their attempts to reconstruct Donner's death. Against the background of snore-like buzzing, we hear stealthy footsteps and a creaking board. Both sounds stop before Donner is heard saying, 'Ah! There you are'. Two quick steps are followed by a thump, a cry, and the noises he makes as he falls through the balustrade to land at the bottom of the stairs. According to Beauchamp, he must have been woken by Martello, who must have murdered him. Martello, who knows that he didn't, assumes Beauchamp was the murderer. It is natural for the audience to begin by assuming that one of them is telling the truth and the other lying, but it is revealed in the end that Donner was not asleep, that the first noise was not a snore but the buzzing of a fly, that the footsteps were Donner's, that the words were addressed to the fly, that the thump was made by his attempt to swat it, and that he lost his balance. Stoppard's intricate design pivots around the ambiguity of a sound effect.

The central event in the trio's past is also based on ambiguous evidence, which has probably been misinterpreted. Seeing the three young artists at an exhibition of their work, Sophie, a beautiful girl on the verge of blindness, falls in love with one of them. The question is which one. Meeting them after her loss of sight is complete, she tries to find out who it was she had seen posing for a photographer against a snow scene. Beauchamp, who had painted a border fence in the snow, becomes her lover, but he does not want to marry her and the affair ends in her death. Donner has consistently been much more deeply interested in her than Beauchamp, whose attitude to art has less in common with hers than Donner's has. The ironical climax of the penultimate sequence is the revelation that Donner may have been the man who attracted her. With her failing sight, she may have mistaken his painting of white posts for a snow scene: when Beauchamp mentioned his fence, she probably misconstrued her memory of the dark gaps between the posts.

Sophie's mistake depends partly on inaccuracy in interpreting perceptual evidence and partly on inaccuracy in remembering it. The two forms of vagueness often overlap, and in personal relationships, blurred memories of past behaviour help us to misinterpret each other's current intentions. Stoppard has a keen eye for the comedy to be tapped from these sources, and in the first three sequences he makes good use of the old men's failing memories. Martello and Beauchamp argue about whether it was Augustus John or Edith Sitwell who used to say, 'If Donner whistles the opening of Beethoven's Fifth in six/eight time once more I'll *kill* him!' (That Martello is the first to mention this irritating habit is a red herring reminiscent of *The Real Inspector Hound,* in which everyone except the real murderer made homicidal threats.) Edith Sitwell features in several of the arguments about the past:

> DONNER: It was Lewis who said that.
> BEAUCHAMP: Lewis who?
> DONNER: Wyndham Lewis.
> BEAUCHAMP: It was Edith Sitwell, as a matter of fact.
> DONNER: Rubbish.
> BEAUCHAMP: She came out with it while we were dancing.
> DONNER: You never danced with Edith Sitwell.
> BEAUCHAMP: Oh yes I did.

DONNER: You're thinking of that American woman who sang negro spirituals at Nancy Cunard's coming-out ball.
BEAUCHAMP: It was Queen Mary's wedding, as a matter of fact.
DONNER: You're mad.
BEAUCHAMP: I don't mean wedding, I mean launching.

And best of all, there is Edith's encounter with Lenin in Zurich: 'Edith saw through him right away. She said to him, "Don't know what you're waiting for but it's not going to happen in Switzerland".'

The first mention of Zurich brings us even closer to the muddled memories of *Travesties:*

BEAUCHAMP: In Zurich in 1915 you told Tarzan he was too conservative.
DONNER: Tarzan?
BEAUCHAMP: I don't mean Tarzan. Who do I mean? Similar name, conservative, 1915 . . .
DONNER: Tsar Nicholas?
BEAUCHAMP: No, no, Zurich.
DONNER: I remember Zurich . . . after our walking tour.

The continental walking tour will be dramatized in the central flashback. Martello has an Uncle Rupert in the War Office, whose advice is that the shooting of Archduke Ferdinand does not constitute a reason for changing their plans. 'There will be no war for the very good reason that His Majesty's Government is not *ready* to go to war, and it will be six months at least before we are strong enough to beat the French.' Predisposed to believe that an uncle in the War Office cannot be wrong, they gaily go to France, where they gaily misinterpret the indications that war has already begun. The explosions in the distance must be quarrying. Even if the men digging a ditch are soldiers, perhaps they are laying pipes.

The scheme of the play, with its V-shaped movement into the past, is eminently suitable for radio, while Stoppard (like Beckett in *All That Fall*) makes good use of a blind character, who (like the audience) needs to be kept informed about what is

Tom Stoppard

going on. The ninth sequence, which will culminate in Sophie's death, consists entirely of a tortured monologue. Abandoned by Beauchamp, she is talking to Donner, who wants her to live with him:

> And who will light the fire; and choose my clothes so the colours don't clash; and find my other shoe; and do up my dress at the back? You haven't thought about it. And if you have then you must think that I will be your lover. But I will not. I cannot. And I cannot live with you knowing that you want me—Do you see that? . . . Mouse? Are you here? Say something. Now, don't do that, Mouse, it's not fair—please, you are here . . . Did you go out? Now please don't . . . How can I do anything if I can't trust you—I beg you, if you're here, tell me. What do you want? Are you just going to watch me?—standing quietly in the room—sitting on the bed—on the edge of the tub—Watch me move about the room, grieving, talking to myself, sleeping, washing, dressing, undressing, crying?—Oh no, there is no way now—I won't—I won't—I won't—no, I won't . . .!
> *(Glass panes and wood smash violently. Silence. In the silence, hoofbeats, in the street, then her body hitting, a horse neighing.)*

This is no less intense than the intensest writing in *Where Are They Now?* but it sits more comfortably in its context.

TRAVESTIES

The convention of the flashback is that it represents past events as they actually occurred: it is always unsatisfactory because it always implies that the brain is a library that contains accurate records of all past experience. All you have to do is find the right shelf. But as Beckett argues in his study of Proust, the remembering consciousness 'has no interest in the mysterious element of inattention that colours our most commonplace experiences. It presents the past in monochrome. The images it chooses are as arbitrary as those chosen by imagination, and are equally remote from reality.' From this point of view, the arguments in *Artist Descending a Staircase* about Edith Sitwell, Lenin and Tristan Tzara are more satisfactory than the flashbacks, for which the play implicitly claims objectivity.

In *Travesties* Stoppard goes on to devise a method of incorporating the distortions of memory into the picture of the past. As he puts it in a stage direction, most of the play 'is under the erratic control of Old Carr's memory, which is not notably reliable, and also of his various prejudices and delusions. One result is that the story (like a toy train perhaps) occasionally jumps the rails and has to be restarted at the point where it goes wild.' Stoppard uses the phrase 'time slips' for the passages where the needle of Carr's unreliable memory sticks in a groove of the past. In the first scene with Bennett[1] (another Wildean manservant like Birdboot in *Lord Malquist and Mr Moon*) the exchange

> BENNETT: Yes, sir. I have put the newspapers and telegrams on the sideboard, sir.

---

[1] Bennett was actually the name of the British Consul in Zurich. Annoyed by his unhelpfulness over the amateur production of *The Importance of Being Earnest,* Joyce wrote a limerick about him and later used his name for the sergeant-major mentioned in the brothel sequence of *Ulysses.* Carr's name is given to the private.

John Wood as Henry Carr in the Royal Shakespeare Company's production of *Travesties* at the Aldwych Theatre.

CARR: Is there anything of interest?

occurs five times within six pages, but the dialogue continues into a different direction each time. Later, in Carr's attempts to reconstruct his first meeting with Cecily, we loop back twice to their exchange:

> I don't think you ought to talk to me like that during library hours. However as the reference section is about to close for lunch I will overlook it. Intellectual curiosity is not so common that one can afford to discourage it. What kind of books were you wanting?
> CARR: Any kind at all.

In an interview published in *The Times*[1] just before the play opened at the Aldwych, Peter Wood, the director, remarked on its

> resemblance to Nabokov's *Pale Fire* in that it's narrated by an extraordinary, erratic old gentleman who has (a) a poor memory, (b) powerful reactionary prejudices, and (c) a high sense of fantasy . . . It's a view of history seen prismatically through the vision of Henry Carr. At one point Tom was thinking of calling it *Prism*.

It is also a continuation of the argument about art that ran through *Artist Descending a Staircase*. Like Beauchamp, Tristan Tzara is a representative of the attitude that 'Nowadays an artist is someone who makes art mean the things he does. A man may be an artist by exhibiting his hindquarters. He may be a poet by drawing words out of a hat'. Carr's riposte echoes Donner:

> An artist is someone who is gifted in some way that enables him to do something more or less well which can only be done badly or not at all by someone who is not thus gifted. If there is any point in using language at all it is that a word is taken to stand for a particular fact or idea and not for other facts or ideas . . . Don't you see my dear Tristan you are simply asking me to accept that the word Art means whatever you wish it to mean; but I do not accept it.

[1]   8 June 1974.

Tom Stoppard

Stoppard's private anxieties about the uselessness of art[1] found their way into the radio play when Donner argued that the war made nonsense of the artistic activity:

> We tried to make a distinction between the art that celebrated reason and history and logic and all assumptions, and our own dislocated anti-art of lost faith—but it was all the same insult to a one-legged soldier and the one-legged, one-armed, one-eyed regiment of the maimed. And here we are still at it, looking for another twist.

One of the points Stoppard enjoyed most of all in the performance of *Travesties* was the audience's audibly enthusiastic response to Carr's envious denunciation of the artist:

> When I was at school, on certain afternoons we all had to do what was called Labour—weeding, sweeping, sawing logs for the boiler-room, that kind of thing; but if you had a chit from Matron you were let off to spend the afternoon messing about in the Art Room. Labour or Art. And you've got a chit for life. *(Passionately) Where d'you get it?* What is an artist? For every thousand people there's 900 doing the work, 90 doing well, nine doing good, and one lucky bastard who's the artist.

The final sentence is another verbatim echo of *Artist Descending a Staircase.*

The presence of Lenin in *Travesties* challenges the significance of Joyce and Tzara. All three were revolutionaries, but how much do artistic revolutions ultimately matter? Joyce, whose answer to this question is similar to Wilde's, argues that the artist is

> the magician put among men to gratify—capriciously—their urge for immortality . . . If there is any meaning in any of it, it is in what survives as art, yes even in the celebration of tyrants, yes even in the celebration of nonentities. What now

[1] cf. Interview, page 2.

118

of the Trojan War if it had been passed over by the artist's touch? Dust. A forgotten expedition prompted by Greek merchants looking for new markets. A minor redistribution of broken pots.

And the curtain line of Act One is Carr's recollection of a question he put to Joyce:

'And what did you do in the Great War?' 'I wrote Ulysses,' he said. 'What did you do?' Bloody nerve.

The Importance of Being Earnest is used in more or less the same kind of way that *Hamlet* was in *Rosencrantz and Guildenstern Are Dead,* but in this palimpsest most of the original writing has been rubbed out. The only quotation which is presented as such is a few lines of dialogue which Carr speaks off-stage. But the echoes, allusions and parallels are intricate, and, as in *Lord Malquist and Mr Moon,* one of the main subjects is a conflict of style. The Wildean element evokes a vanished elegance. 1918 serves as a point not quite midway between the debonair nineties and the less glamorous present. Wilde died eighteen years too early to be introduced as a character, and Stoppard no longer needs to introduce an anachronistic modern equivalent, such as Lord Malquist. The action is built around a series of collisions between contrasted styles of behaviour, conflicting artistic programmes and conflicting views on whether style is in itself something to be valued.

Except that Lenin and Tzara were both (on neutral ground) in Zurich when James Joyce involved a British consular official called Henry Carr in an amateur production of *The Importance,* there is no historical jusification for bringing the four figures together, but of course no better historical justification is needed, and Stoppard has created a clever theatrical equation between Tzara and Jack Worthing.[1] We learn from Bennett that a Mr Tzara has left his card and he is an artist. Carr administers

[1] Tristan Tzara was itself a pseudonym. His real name was Sami Rosenstock.

Tom Stoppard

a Wildean reproof: 'I will not have you passing moral judgements on my friends. If Mr Tzara is an artist that is his misfortune.' Soon Tzara presents himself, announcing in an outrageous Rumanian accent that he wants to marry Henry's sister Gwendolen. Thanks to a time slip he makes the same entrance ten minues later, this time without the accent. The ensuing conversation is pastiche of Wilde peppered with good Stoppardian puns and new variations on the old theme of accident and causality:

> TZARA: Eating and drinking, as usual, I see, Henry? I have often observed that Stoical principles are more easily borne by those Epicurean habits.
>
> CARR (*stiffly*): I believe it is done to drink a glass of hock and seltzer before luncheon, and it is well done to drink it well before luncheon. I took to drinking hock and seltzer for my nerves at a time when nerves were fashionable in good society. This season it is trenchfoot, but I drink it regardless because I feel much better after it.
>
> TZARA: You might have felt much better anyway.
>
> CARR: No, no—post hock, propter hock.
>
> TZARA: But, my dear Henry, causality is no longer fashionable owing to the war.
>
> CARR: How illogical, since the war itself had causes. I forget what they were, but it was all in the papers at the time.

Tzara, already committed (like Duchamp and Mallarmé) to the artistic principles that were later to be dubbed 'aleatory', employs a polished nineties style to advance an anti-Style argument:

> The clever people try to impose a design on the world and when it goes calamitously wrong they call it fate. In point of fact, everything is Chance, including design . . . the causes we know everything about depend on causes we know absolutely nothing about. And it is the duty of the artist to jeer and howl and belch at the delusion that infinite generations of real effects can be inferred from the gross expression of apparent cause.

The association of Tzara with Jack Worthing is strengthened by the use of Joyce as Lady Bracknell and by the part of the plot that deals with the library ticket. Cecily, the librarian, is an admirer of Lenin, who introduced Tzara to her. This is how he later describes the meeting:

> 'Tzara!' said she. 'Not the Dadaist, I hope!' 'My younger brother, Tristan,' I replied. 'Most unfortunate. Terrible blow to the family.' When I filled up my application form, for some reason the first name I thought of was Jack.

In Gwendolen's declaration of love to Tzara, the first two sentences are identical to two sentences in the other Gwendolen's declaration to Jack Worthing:

> For me you have always had an irresistible fascination. Even before I met you I was far from indifferent to you.

The last sentence of the speech in *The Importance* is:

> The moment Algernon first mentioned to me that he had a friend called Ernest, I knew I was destined to love you.

The last sentence of her speech in *Travesties* is:

> When Henry told me that he had a friend who edited a magazine of all that is newest and best in literature, I knew I was destined to love you.

Wilde's Gwendolen says that she would be unable to love Jack if his name were not Ernest; Stoppard's Gwendolen would be unable to love Tzara if he did not admire Joyce's work.

There may be an element of comically concealed autobiography in infiltrating a Slav writer into the Englishness of languid epigrams and tea-parties with cucumber sandwiches. Certainly there is theatrical potential in the stylistic clash between the two Irishmen who preside over the play. Wilde became exorbitantly English; Joyce became European. Stoppard pays tribute to his polyglot vocabulary with the library scene that opens the play. For several very amusing minutes, not a single sentence of standard English is spoken. Tzara reads from the poem he is composing by means of cut-up techniques; Joyce dictates an incomprehensible mixture of English, German, Latin, nonsense and neologisms, with Gwendolen echoing almost everything he says; Lenin and his wife converse in Russian. Cecily keeps coming in to say 'Sssssssh!'.

Travesties repeats the pattern of *The Real Inspector Hound* in making a play-within-a-play entangle outsiders not only into its style but into its events. Playing Algernon in the amateur production of *The Importance,* Carr is drawn into an equally Wildean relationship with Cecily. Arriving at the library to spy on Lenin, Carr introduces himself by presenting Tzara's card. (Like a goldfish, a visiting-card that is used once must be used twice.) It gives Tzara's Christian name as Tristan, so Cecily takes Carr to be the 'decadent nihilist' who is the younger brother of the man she knows as Jack Tzara. Nevertheless she finds a point of affinity. Like Constance in *'M' Is for Moon among Other Things*, who reads alphabetically through the monthly instalments of the encyclopaedia, Cecily is educating herself by working her way along the library shelves. Impressed that Mr Tzara asks to borrow any book at all, she enquires whether there is no limit to the scope of his interests:

> CARR: It is rather that I wish to increase it. An overly methodical education has left me to fend as best I can with some small knowledge of the aardvark, a mastery of the abacus and a facility for abstract art. An aardvark, by the way, is a sort of African pig found mainly—
>
> CECILY: I know only too well what an aardvark is, Mr Tzara. To be frank, you strike a sympathetic chord in me.
>
> CARR: Politically, I haven't really got beyond anarchism.
>
> CECILY: I see. Your elder brother, meanwhile—
>
> CARR: Bolshevism. And you, I suppose . . .?
>
> CECILY: Zimmervaldism!

Stoppard exploits the confusion of identity to advance his plot. Not knowing that she is talking to the British Consul—Carr was only a consular official but his memory has promoted him—Cecily divulges that Bennett, who has radical sympathies, has been leaking the secrets of consular correspondence to Mr Jack Tzara:

> CECILY: Oh dear, there I go again! You are not a bit like your brother. You are more English.
> CARR: I assure you I am as Bulgarian as he is.
> CECILY: He is Rumanian.
> CARR: They are the same place. Some people call it the one, some the other.
> CECILY: I didn't know that, though I always suspected it.

Like so many of the other conversations, this one develops into an argument about art, Cecily taking the view that 'The sole duty and justification for art is social criticism . . . we live in an age when the social order is seen to be the work of material forces and we have been given an entirely new kind of responsibility, the responsibility of changing society.' Carr is much closer to sharing the view that Wilde expressed in his duologue *The Critic as Artist—with Some Remarks on the Importance of Doing Nothing*. The connection with *The Importance of Being Earnest* is emphasized by naming one of the characters Ernest. The main speaker, Gilbert, insists that 'emotion for the sake of emotion is the aim of art, and emotion for the sake of action is the aim of life, and of that practical organization of life that we call society . . . The sure way of knowing nothing about life is to try to make oneself useful.' The one duty we owe to history, he says, is to rewrite it.

He maintains that 'To arrive at what one really believes, one must speak through lips different from one's own'—a sentence Stoppard could have emblazoned on his banner, if he needed one. In *Travesties* he draws on Shakespeare, Wilde, Joyce, Tzara and Lenin. Parodying Joyce's device of switching from one style to another in mid-narrative, he imitates the catechism sequence in *Ulysses* by writing a long sequence in which Tzara answers Joyce's Bracknellish questions about Dada. The syntax is sometimes Wildean, sometimes Joycean, sometimes Dadaistic. Another sequence is written in limericks, with each one split between several characters, and there is another sequence in rhyme that can be sung by Gwendolen and Cecily in the manner of 'Mr Gallagher and Mr Shean'. Believing themselves to be in love with the same Tzara, the two girls express their waspish hostility until the confusion is resolved in the last three words.

> GWEN: Miss Carruthers,
>   Is it done to wish you luck with all the others?
>   I'm not awfully au fait
>   with manners down you way—
> CECILY: And up yours, Miss Carr—Tristan!
>   (CARR *has entered. Pause*)
> GWEN (*censoriously*): That's my brother.

Stoppard succeeds with all his stylistic variations except the lecture at the beginning of the second act.[1] The chief reason for its failure is that its main function is to provide background information about Marxism and Lenin. This is not compatible with advancing the action. The problem could possibly have been solved by making Lenin less prominent, but it would have been a mistake to cut him out of the play. He usefully personifies the political reality which in *Artist Descending a Staircase* was represented by the war and in *Jumpers* by the Rad Libs. His presence also makes it possible for Stoppard to contrive some effective contrasts and shifts. For instance, Carr's sexual fantasies about Cecily are theatricalized with coloured lights flickering over her body while a big band plays 'The Stripper', until we move abruptly to a Lenin sequence which makes political revolutionaries look no less absurd that British consular officials or artists. In March 1917, unable to return legally to Russia with Zinoviev, Lenin writes to Yakov Ganetsky in Stockholm:

> The only possible plan is as follows: you must find two Swedes who resemble Zinoviev and me, but since we cannot speak Swedish they must be deaf mutes. I enclose our photograph for this purpose.

The equally absurd contradictions in his attitude to art can be

[1] See Interview, page 9.

exposed by direct quotation:

> Aren't you ashamed for printing 5,000 copies of Mayakovsky's new book? It is nonsense, stupidity, double-dyed stupidity and affectation. I believe such things should be published one in ten, and not more than 1,500 copies, for librarians and cranks! I can't listen to music often. It affects my nerves, makes me want to say nice stupid things and pat the heads of those people who while living in this vile hell can create such beauty. Nowadays we can't pat heads or we'll get our hands bitten off. We've got to *hit* heads, hit them without mercy, though ideally we're against doing violence to people.

But the treatment of Lenin comes uneasily and unnecessarily close to historical accuracy. It might have been better if Stoppard could have relaxed into allowing himself the same liberties that he takes with Joyce and Tzara. One of the best jokes in the Lenin plot is a more theatrical variation of the Uncle Rupert joke we had in *Artist Descending a Staircase*. After Lenin and his wife have left for Russia on the train, Carr, who has been preoccupied with amateur dramatics, decides to take action:

> He must be stopped. The Russians have got a government of patriotic and moderate men. Prince Lvov is moderately conservative, Kerensky is moderately socialist, and Guchkov is a businessman. All in all a promising foundation for a liberal democracy on the Western model, and for a vigorous prosecution of the war on the Eastern front, followed by a rapid expansion of trade.

According to Cecily, when we meet her as an old woman in the closing sequence, Carr never even set eyes on Lenin, but according to him

> I'd got pretty close to him . . . and I'd got a pretty good idea of his plans, in fact I might have stopped the whole Bolshevik thing in its tracks, but—here's the point. I was uncertain. What was the right thing? And then there were

my feelings for Cecily. And don't forget, *he wasn't Lenin then! I mean who was he?* as it were.

The old man even confuses his manservant with the British Consul. For the final curtain Stoppard uses a joke from Charlie's speech in *Dogg's Our Pet,* but it now works to much greater effect as a pleasantly inconclusive conclusion to a play which has already said a great deal about forgetfulness:

> I learned three things in Zurich during the war. I wrote them down. Firstly, you're either a revolutionary or you're not, and if you're not you might as well be an artist as anything else. Secondly, if you can't be an artist, you might as well be a revolutionary . . . I forget the third thing.

Although Tzara and Joyce are both accommodated more comfortably than Lenin into the scheme of the play, Stoppard does not pick up all the cues that Dada and Joyce offer him for trying out new kinds of theatrical writing. *Travesties* has some incidental affinities with Roger Vitrac's *Les Mystères de l'Amour,* which Martin Esslin[1] describes as 'probably the most sustained effort to write a truly Surrealist play'. Its characters include Lloyd George and Mussolini; the action absorbs fantasies into the flow of events; several locales are represented simultaneously on the same playing area. Stoppard's original idea was to have the library on one side of the set and Carr's room on the other; Peter Wood's production took one step towards Surrealism by merging the two.

The joyful proliferation of parodies creates a mood comparable to the iconoclastic exuberance of the Dadaists. In *Dada Art and Anti-Art,* one of the books Stoppard used, Hans Richter assumed that the name Dada had a connection

> with the joyous Slavonic affirmative 'da, da'—and to me this seemed wholly appropriate. Nothing could better express our optimism, our sensation of newly-won freedom, than this powerfully reiterated 'da, da'—'yes, yes' to life.

[1] *The Theatre of the Absurd*, Eyre and Spottiswode.

Whirling on the merry-go-round of Stoppard's satirical inspiration, the audience feels pleasantly dizzy, but this dizziness is very different from the vertigo of the early plays and from the vertigo of the Surrealists and Dadaists, who were torn between obstreperous infantilism and didacticism. The murderous politicians must be given a cautionary lesson in irresponsibility. This is why the work of art was always threatening to topple over the brink of madness, nonsense, silence, annihilation. Artaud considered suicide as the only means of using willpower to impose a design on the chaos of life. The architectonic virtuosity of the mature Stoppard is a satisfying distraction from the *Angst* in the early work. Fluency fills the void. Though possibly he could answer in the same way as Vitrac, who wrote himself into *Les Mystères de l'Amour* to argue with the romantic hero when he complains about the words of love that have been put into his mouth. He tried to spit them out, he says, but they turned into bullets or into vertigo. 'That's not my fault,' says the author. 'That's what life is like.'

Life—or the passage of time—has given us an image of James Joyce very different from the one he had of himself, and there is much to be said in favour of creating a new image to be sighted through a prism of conflicting styles and memories. My main reservation is about language. There are some appealingly Joycean puns in *Travesties*—'empirical purple', 'ulterior violets', 'the joyce of spring', 'the yesnos of yesteryear' and 'mucus mutandis' as a gloss on 'snot-green'. But the dialogue never becomes as Joycean as it did in one of Archie's speeches in the dreamlike Coda of *Jumpers*:

> Indeed, if moon mad herd instinct, is God dad the inference?—to take another point: If goons in mood, by Gad is sin different or banned good, f'r'instance?—thirdly: out of the ether, random nucleic acid testes or neither universa vice, to name but one—fourthly: If the necessary being isn't, surely mother of invention as Voltaire said, not to mention Darwin different from the origin of the specious—to sum up: Super, both natural and stitious, sexual ergo cogito er go-go sometimes, as Descartes said, and who are we?

A whole play in this idiom would be intolerable, but it will be a pity if Stoppard does not, sooner or later, come seriously to grips with the Joycean style. It would be interesting if he wrote a play in which Joyce and Beckett were the two main characters, silence swimming in the stream of consciousness. So far, one of the differences between Beckett and Stoppard is that Beckett conveys the worrying impression that at any second the words could crumble into non-existence. With Stoppard we feel a relaxed confidence that the flow of words, jokes, parodies, ideas is inexhaustible. The effort behind the writing remains invisible. It may be that he is not going out of his way to hide it, but what would happen if he revealed it?

DIRTY LINEN and
NEW-FOUND-LAND

To celebrate his naturalization as a British subject and the 200th anniversary of the American Revolt, Ed Berman commissioned Stoppard to write the first in a series of new plays to be staged at the Almost Free Theatre under the title *The American Connection*. The authors were free to choose their own way of introducing the American theme. Having started on *Dirty Linen*, Stoppard found that it was developing into something which had no connection either with Ed Berman or with the United States, but which was too good to scrap. The solution was to write a shorter play, *New-Found-Land*, which could be interpolated, like an entr'acte, between the two halves of *Dirty Linen*. The plays are set in the same locale, a room in the tower of Big Ben, and they are seamed neatly together with small overlaps. Except for one beautiful nymphomaniac, the characters are all Members of Parliament. The room is used for meetings of Commons committees, and the stage vibrates with booming chimes at intervals of fifteen minutes.

Both plays are lightweight in comparison with Stoppard's two previous one-acters for Inter-Action, but they work no less efficiently as laughter-raisers. Like *Travesties, Dirty Linen* begins as if Stoppard had set himself the task of finding out how many minutes of comic dialogue he could write without introducing a single phrase of straightforward English. After trying to hang their bowler hats on the same hook, McTeazle and Cocklebury-Smythe sustain a long and very funny conversation in French, Latin and Spanish tags. The first words of English, 'Bloody awkward though', are excused by 'Pardon my French'.

Increasing technical know-how encourages a playwright to be increasingly unhurried about explaining his basic situation. Far from needing to understand the reasons for everything that is going on, audiences respond happily to mystification and to discreet sexual titillation. Stoppard builds up slowly to the revelation that both men are members of a Select Committee which has been set up to investigate the rumours about a Mystery Woman who has side-tracked seventeen Members from the path of virtue. Since then many more have succumbed. As McTeazle sums it up:

> we face the possibility that a sexual swathe has passed through Westminster claiming the reputations of, to put no finer point on it, 119 Members. Someone is going through the ranks like a lawnmower in knickers.

By now it is clear that both men are anxious that Maddie Gotobed, the suspiciously attractive and suspiciously incompetent stenographer, should say nothing about the time they have been spending with her. Immediately after her first entrance, she put on a pair of knickers which she took out of a shopping bag, and during the first few minutes of the action, both men covertly return to her the knickers they have brought along. One meaning of the title is already clear.

The dialogue is full of innuendoes such as

> we as a Committee are working in a sensitive area, one which demands great tact on all our parts

Freudian slips such as

> why don't you have a quick poke, peek, in the Members' Bra—or the cafeteria, they're probably guzzling coffee and Swedish panties, (MADDIE *has crossed her legs)* Danish

and exchanges such as

> McTEAZLE: I expect it's not every girl who proves herself as you have done, Miss Gotobed. Do you use Greggs or do you favour the Pitman method?
> MADDIE: I'm on the pill.

There are also some three-dimensional puns. The Chairman of the Committee, who tries to help Maddie by writing on the blackboard for her, wipes it clean with a pair of lace-trimmed knickers which he produces from his briefcase. He stows them away quickly but not quite quickly enough:

What is *that*?
Pair of briefs.
What are they doing in there?
It's a brief case.

On the evidence of the play, Stoppard does not feel very strongly about the moral irresponsibility of MPs. The themes that do preoccupy him seriously are mostly absent from this play, though occasionally we hear a familiar motif in the dialogue. The argument in *Artist Descending a Staircase* and in *Travesties* about whether anyone can make himself into an artist just by calling the things he makes 'art', is comically echoed in Cocklebury-Smythe's doubts about whether a Prime Minister can make a commoner into a real peer:

> He said to me 'my dear Cockie, life peers *are* the real thing nowadays'. 'Oh no they're not, Rollo' I said. 'That's just the kind of confusion you set up in people's minds by calling them Lord This and Lord That, pour encourager hoi polloi. *They* think they're lords—they skip off home and feed the budgerigar saying to themselves, My golly gorblimey, I'm a lord! They'd be just as happy if you suddenly told them they were all sheiks. They'd put the Desert Song on the gramophone and clap their hands when they wanted their cocoa. Now *you'd* know they're not really sheiks and I'd know they're not really sheiks, and God help them if they ever showed up east of Suez in their appalling pullovers with Sheik Shuttleworth stencilled on their airline bags—no, my dear Rollo,' I said, 'I'll be a real peer or not at all.' 'Now look here, Cockie,' he said to me, 'If they weren't real peers they wouldn't be in the House of Lords would they?—that's logic.' 'If that's logic,' I said, 'you can turn a regimental goat into a Lieutenant Colonel by electing it to the United Services Club.'

This time the committee consists of six Members and one of them is a woman, but as with the male quartets of *If You're Glad I'll Be Frank* and *Albert's Bridge*, Stoppard is setting a reactionary conformism in opposition to an individualistic

131

rebellion, while the committee members always defend themselves against evidence of corruption with pompous reiterations of the word 'irreproachable'. Stoppard does not identify with Maddie as much as he did with Glad, with Frank and with Albert, but he ironically puts the most intelligent argument into the mouth of the girl who is required by protocol to keep it shut:

> MADDIE: The press. The more you accuse them of malice and inaccuracy, the more you're admitting that they've got a right to poke their noses into your private life. All this fuss! The whole report can go straight into the waste paper basket. All you need is just one paragraph saying that MPs have got just as much right to enjoy themselves in their own way as anyone else, and Fleet Street can take a running jump.
>
> WITHENSHAW: Miss Gotobed, you may not be aware that the clerk traditionally refrains from drafting the report of a Select Committee.
>
> MADDIE: And anyway, there's no malice in it. You've got that wrong, too.

The structural joke is that the committee is forced into going along with Maddie's ideas. Withenshaw, who expects a peerage if he produces the report that the Prime Minister wants, is confronted with a dangerous-seeming challenge from French, who appears to be the one incorruptible member of the committee. He consistently votes against the majority and on Friday he had tea with the Dean of St Paul's. Left alone with Maddie at the adjournment, he tells her, 'Miss Gotobed, this is going to teach them a lesson they'll never forget'. In the last line spoken before the stage is cleared for *New-Found-Land* she asks him to show her the way to the ladies' cloakroom and in the final sequence of *Dirty Linen* he is not only using her new pair of knickers to mop at his sweating brow, he forces the committee to scrap the Chairman's draft, replacing it with a much shorter report, which says what Maddie wants it to.

New-Found-Land may depend mainly on anecdote and monologue, but it contains a delightful characterization of the man who tells the anecdote. He is a deaf and bumbling Home Office official who finds it hard to concentrate on anything but the story of how, as a boy, he won £5 off Lloyd George. The Prime Minister gained access to the upstairs room where the boy's mother was in bed by betting that he would be able to see Big Ben from the window. The clock was visible but the boy won his point by insisting that Big Ben was the name of the bell. The Prime Minister did not subsequently regret the outlay.

A junior official is trying to make the old man focus his attention on the question of whether British nationality should be granted to a bearded applicant who is associated with a farm in Kentish Town, has an income of £10.50 a week, runs some sort of bus service, has an interest in publishing, writes plays and wants to be British because he is American. This is sufficient cue for both officials to make speeches about America. The old actor makes a short speech, at the end of which he goes to sleep. The young actor, who so far has not been much more than a stooge-like straight man, is now rewarded with an immensely long, extremely funny speech, clotted with travelogue clichés, literary allusions and metaphysical conceits that might have been squeezed through the censorship of a Hollywood script editor.

> Snow-capped mountains shimmer on the horizon, and still we climb. From the observation platform at the rear we watch the shadows turn the thousand-foot walls of the Colorado River deep red and purple. Huddled in our blanket we sleep. Once we seem to wake to a nightmare of acrylic lights—against a magenta sky huge electric horseshoes, dice, roulette wheels and giant Amazons with tasselled breasts change colour atop marble citadels that would beggar Kubla Khan. But when the cheerful Redcap shakes us all is peace. The Silver Chief is rolling through vineyards and orchards, a sun bathed Canaan decked with peach and apricot, apples, plums, citrus fruit and pomegranates, which grow to the very walls of pink and yellow bungalows, to the very edge of swimming pools where near-naked goddesses with honey-brown skins rub oil into their long downy limbs. Could this be paradise?—or is

it after all, purgatory?—for look!—there, where movie palaces rise from the plain, searchlights and letters of fire light up the sky, and a screaming hydra-headed mob surges, fighting and weeping, around an unseen idol—golden calf or cadillac, we do not stop to see—for now beyond the city, beyond America, beyond all, nothing lies before us but an endless expanse of blue, flecked with cheerful whitecaps.

It is a virtuoso piece of writing, highly theatrical in its way of playing with the audience expectations that the comic rhetoric arouses, highly untheatrical in having only the slightest of connections with this slightest of stories.

EVERY GOOD BOY DESERVES
FAVOUR and PROFESSIONAL FOUL

The erosion of individual liberty in the Communist countries is a subject which had grown unfashionable among British playwrights as Left Wing didacticism became dominant, but after visiting Moscow and Leningrad in February 1977, Tom Stoppard was impelled to write about what he had witnessed. He had already accepted a commission from André Previn to script a play for performance in a concert hall by actors and a symphony orchestra. After seeing how the Soviet Ministry of Internal Affairs and the KGB use mental hospitals as prisons, Stoppard decided to write about a dissident who finds himself in the same cell as a man with hallucinations about having his own symphony orchestra. The situation is farcically complicated by making the asylum's doctor a keen amateur violinist who plays in an orchestra. So the eighty musicians on the platform sometimes represent a real orchestra and sometimes an orchestra that has no existence outside the lunatic's head, while the full blast of orchestral sound we hear sometimes represents sounds inaudible to anyone but him.

Not that these are the only ways Stoppard has found of integrating the orchestra into his play. There is musical parody of movement, the oboe mimicking the awkwardness of the doctor as he hurries between his office and his place in the orchestra. There is incidental music, music to bridge between two sequences, music to back speech, singing, ironical musical illustration (Tchaikovsky's 1812 Overture), and sabotage of orchestral unity by a dissident instrument. The lunatic plays his real triangle either in tempo with his imaginary orchestra or manically out of tempo. There is also a sequence in which the musicians look as though they are playing, but no sound is emitted: bows are not quite touching strings, no air is being blown into wind instruments. As in the *Jumpers* sequence when we see a vase being dropped but hear the noise of a trumpet being kicked down a flight of stairs,[1] Stoppard is exploring

[1] See pages 107–8.

the possibility of conflict between stage picture and accompanying sound.

Without betraying the gravity of his subject by the frivolity of his treatment, he uses farce to expose some of the absurdities in the equation of dissidence with insanity. In the USSR, the authority of doctors is subordinate to that of state officials—a situation which is incompatible with high medical standards. Stoppard found a member of Amnesty, currently serving seven years in a labour camp, who had refused to undergo an operation for a rectal tumour, distrusting the surgeons in the camp hospital. In *Every Good Boy Deserves Favour* the doctor, who kowtows to the commissars, has little to offer his patients except brightly coloured pills. Insisting that the dissident is a schizophrenic, he promises to cure him by seven o'clock on Tuesday evening, with the aid of a mild laxative. 'The layman often doesn't realize that medicine advances in a series of imaginative leaps.'

The television play *Professional Foul* contains less farce, less comedy and more straightforward treatment of the human suffering inflicted by totalitarian regimes. In the opening sequence, set on the aeroplane which is carrying three English philosophy lecturers to an international congress in Prague, there is some jokey argument and some comically fastidious philosophizing in the manner of *Jumpers*, but this is mainly to prepare us for the change in the attitude of the Cambridge Professor of Ethics when he is brought face to face with the cruelty of the state's subordination of human reality to a fiction about a collective ethic.

In Leningrad Stoppard met a man who had graduated in English Literature but had to work as a part-time lift-operator; in the television play, Professor Anderson is visited in his Prague hotel by a former pupil, Hollar, who is working as a lavatory cleaner, in spite of having a Cambridge First in Philosophy. Asked to smuggle a doctoral thesis to England for him, Anderson at first reacts by saying that as a guest of the government, he cannot repay hospitality with behaviour that would be unethical. He is even reluctant to believe that the hotel bedrooms are bugged. But when he goes to Hollar's flat, the police are searching it. Hollar has been arrested and, finding nothing incriminating, the policemen plant a package of dollars to substantiate an accusation about a currency offence. Abandoning his prepared paper, Anderson lectures the congress about individual rights until the Chairman arranges for a fire alarm to interrupt the session.

The least satisfactory element in the play is the sub-plot about football. The play's title links a calculated foul committed during a game between England and Czechoslovakia with the action of the Czech police in planting the dollars, but the analogy is not very fruitful, though it does produce one effective irony: switching the radio on to hear the commentary about the football match, the government official who is supervising the ransacking of the flat clicks his tongue disapprovingly at the footballer's foul play.

Discounting adaptations of his own and other people's work, Stoppard had previously written only four plays for television— *A Separate Peace, Teeth, Another Moon Called Earth* and *Neutral Ground*. They are less substantial than his plays for radio, less interesting and less experimental, not being designed to stretch or even explore the limitations of the medium. *Professional Foul* is longer (one hour, twenty minutes) and considerably more substantial than any of its four predecessors, while, besides the opening conversation on the aeroplane, there are a few characteristically Stoppardian moments. At the congress, an American academic's speech about ambiguity is immediately followed by a misunderstanding, when Anderson stands up, wanting to leave, and the Chairman misinterprets the movement as indicating that he wants to comment on what has been said.

But if the BBC had presented the play pseudonymously, it would have been identifiable as Stoppard's work only by virtue of a few sequences. Never since *Neutral Ground* (1969) has he made so few attempts to raise laughs. As an indictment of the systematic foul play of Communist governments the play is cogent; as a television narrative it is gripping and often touching, even if there was some sentimentality in the scene where Hollar's son, who has learnt English at school, acts as interpreter between his mother and Anderson. But generally Stoppard depends too heavily on the language barrier to unify his material, and, since his work for stage and radio is so distinctive, it is disappointing to find that when he writes for television, he is content with a script much of which could have been produced by any competent screenwriter.

SECOND INTERVIEW WITH TOM STOPPARD 20 August 1976

Ronald Hayman: *Writing the book I had the feeling of discovering certain patterns, recurrences and what looked like preoccupations bordering on the obsessive, but which were valuable in driving you to write what you did write, especially in the early work. What does it feel like to reconsider the early plays in the light of the later ones?*

Tom Stoppard: It's not really a question of returning to obsessional preoccupations so much as coming across a fruitful dramatic situation and coming back to it because one hasn't properly teased out its potential; man whose wife is in bed in another room, visited by mysterious stranger, for example—I would be inclined to think that there's something very interesting and personal going on, and there's nothing at all that I'm aware of. There are other reiterated things in the plays, such as people constantly getting each other's names wrong. My own view is that it is absolutely nothing to do with my name being changed by deed poll without consultation when I was eight or nine. It meant nothing to me at the time. I don't much mind now.

What I tend to find when I look back are things which I just don't like much any more and which it is now too late to change. It's as though they're dead now. Some of the things don't go bad on me. Most of *Travesties*—not as a structure and a play but speech by speech—still seems to me as good as I can ever get. It's slightly worrying actually. A lot of things in *Travesties* and *Jumpers* seem to me to be the terminus of the particular kind of writing which I can do. I don't see much point in trying to do it again, though I probably will, for want of being able to do anything else. There are a lot of things I would like to change, but the important speeches I wouldn't change at all now. In the case of other speeches in other plays I would like to change a lot or take them out and bury them deep in quicklime.

So one of the aims would be to arrive at the terminus?

Yes, there are different kinds of objectives and I don't think I can do better than I've done with *Travesties* if one is going to write that kind of play in that kind of idiom. In terms of trying to put together serious statement and witty expression, that's as good as I can do it, I think.

What about Jumpers? *What was it like going into rehearsal with it again?*

This is a Friday and last Monday we read through it—first reading, first day of rehearsal—and I found that George's very long monologue at the beginning of the play was pretty well as I wanted it to be. It hasn't begun to putrefy in my mind at all. The question now is I don't know what sort of play I would write. I haven't done a large play since *Travesties*. I've done a little joke play rather quickly—*Dirty Linen* and *New-Found-Land*. I've done a piece to go with an orchestra, which is again serious/funny but based much more on fact. It's not a fabulation. I'm now doing a screenplay of a book by Nabokov—*Despair*—set in Berlin in 1930. I've got one more thing I want to do, which is to write a television play, probably historical, about Czechoslovakia, but what I haven't got anywhere near is what would be for me a true successor to *Jumpers* and *Travesties*, i.e. stage plays with all the stops pulled out.

At home, the other night, we watched *The Linden Tree*. Watching with my wife, we both found that this Priestley play was effective and engrossing and altogether admirable as a television play ought to be, in a way which I don't remember a play being since *When We Are Married*, which is the last Priestley play I saw on television. To say that they're conservative is putting it mildly. We like to think that we've got beyond that sort of family saga, and I found myself sitting on the settee thinking, 'I ought to write a play about a middle-class family having a crisis'. I really wanted to do it. I felt I was sick of flashy mind-projections speaking in long, articulate, witty sentences about the great abstractions. I suddenly thought it would be rather nice to write about a professor or a doctor with a grey-haired wife and a problem child, and the maid comes in with the muffin dish and they talk about the weather a bit.

What would happen if you tried to sit down and do that?

I suppose I'd end up doing something rather different. One doesn't really start with the play written. Many people think that one actually understands what it is that the play's going to be. To use a metaphor that I've used before, people tend to think that you think up a skeleton and that writing the play then consists of putting the flesh on it. But you start with some bones and you work on a finger until the skin and the fingernail are perfect and then you do the next finger and by the time you get to the shoulder, you begin to get a dim idea of whether you're writing a camel or a horse. I might start, thinking 'I will do my J.B. Priestley play this year' and I could end up with something utterly bizarre. I'm just making the point about Priestley that it's somehow quite reassuring that sheer craftsmanship still pays off. Observation, truth, no showing off.

Though a play can be very satisfying without any of those virtues.

Dirty Linen works nicely. But I don't think anybody would pretend it was naturalistic. In fact I had a very sweet letter from the Clerks' Department of the House of Commons, inviting me for a drink and pointing out certain discrepancies between the play and the reality it purports to present. *Dirty Linen* is as unlike *The Linden Tree* in some ways as it is unlike Ionesco.

It also deviated from your starting intention of writing a play about Ed Berman's naturalization. And had you started off with the idea of writing a play about the House of Commons it would be different again.

I suppose so. I had no interest in writing about the House of Commons actually. I wouldn't have written the play at all but for the necessity to fulfil a promise. I also want to write a play for Michael Codron. I think people like Codron and Michael White in their way are as important to the theatre as the

National and the Royal Shakespeare Company. So I said, 'Yes, I'll try and do you a play, Michael'. The silly thing is that even I am thinking in terms of 'a Codron-type play' instead of 'a play'. It would be absurd to write a play for Michael Codron that had twenty-eight characters, but that's merely a commercial consideration. What I mean is that I think: 'Oh well this is a chance to write my West End play, to write *The Linden Tree* or *The Rattigan Version*'.

Could there be some unconscious pressure that persuades you to make promises that will limit your freedom and cut off the space of time in which you're at liberty to write anything you like, regardless of promises to Ed or Michael?

Yes, I suppose there is, but really it's more a matter of mad optimism. I never construct these traps for myself. I work out how long I think I'll need to do the thing I'm doing and I'm liable to say: 'Well, I'll be free in six months and I'd be quite interested to do this'. And I find that in six months everything has gone wrong and I'm not free at all and I'll be free six months after that, by which time two other promises are being stretched to breaking point. At the moment I'm really working far too hard and far too much.

In fact I'm ignoring seven-eighths of the reality which one somehow never quite talks about in interviews, but it's the real reason one gets behind. Yesterday I started work at half past nine in the morning and ended up at five o'clock in the afternoon in a foul mood because I'd been interrupted every twelve minutes by one of my four children or one of their three or four friends or telephone calls and having to talk to applicants to be our housekeeper, our housekeeper having just retired. It's domestic life. I wouldn't have it any other way. I can't bear that sort of monk writer. I knew one once who worked in a garage and they had to slip notes under the door. I think one should stop for the children and not make the children stop for the writing.

I really would very much like to take a sabbatical now for about six months, entirely because I buy about three times as many books as I read, continuously. If I could trim my expenditure, as Mr Micawber recommends, so that it's 6p below my income rather than 6p above it, I might actually stop work for a while. One never quite mentions this but of course it's money as well, isn't it? In the end you have to pay the telephone bill.

I have a love-hate relationship with this mythical figure of the dedicated writer. Isn't there a line in *Man and Superman* about using mother's milk for ink? About 51 per cent of me views this figure with utter contempt and about 49 per cent with total admiration. I also have 51 per cent contempt for the artist who is very serious about himself and ploughs a lonely furrow and occasionally a few pages are released to the millions, and 49 per cent admiration. Conversely, I've got a weakness or a commendable admiration for rather shallow people who knock off a telly play and write a rather good novel and go and interview Castro and write a good poem and a bad poem and give a silly interview and every five years do a really good piece of work as well. That sort of eclectic, trivial person who's very gifted. In a way I catch myself liking those people too much, as if they were sirens on a rock saying, 'Come on, come away from the serious artists'. I never quite know whether I want to be a serious artist or a siren. It's not a condition of good art that you sit in a brown study.

The later plays seem more relaxed and you seem more healthily confident in them that the audience is going to be entertained.

I haven't got much recent experience to go on. I wrote *Dirty Linen* last March over the course of a few weeks, and that was rather a different situation. It's three years since I last wrote a big play, so I don't know how relaxed I'd be about it or how confident about having the audience on the play's side. I think on the whole I never do relax about it. It always is one of the twin preoccupations of writing a play, the other one being to make the play say what you want it to say.

Isn't the long speech at the beginning of the second act of Travesties *an example of a risk you wouldn't have taken five years earlier?*

No, it wasn't a risk, it was a miscalculation. What I was trying to do was write a play which was an anthology of different sorts of play and that was one sort. I mean different kinds of style, different kinds of idiom.

It struck me that what used to happen with simple words, puns, when a word like jumpers *acquires different layers of meaning, happens in* Travesties *with different styles. You're producing a space in which there will be a number of chance encounters not this time between the disparate meanings of a single sound but between different styles. The way they bump up against each other becomes one of the things you're using.*

Yes, I just wanted to dislocate the audience's assumptions every now and again about what kind of style the play was going to be in. Dislocation of an audience's assumptions is an important part of what I like to write. It operates in different ways. Even *Dirty Linen* was in my own mind really a play about presenting a stereotype dumb blonde and dislocating the assumptions about the stereotype—although it's possibly not near enough to the centre of the play's focus to register. The black Irish Catholic Jew in *Malquist and Moon* is all part of the same non-obsessional obsession.

Perhaps it's the same thing that surfaces in a different way with these alphabetical lists that occur both in 'M' is for Moon *and in* Travesties, *when the mere fact of two subjects in an encyclopaedia or in a library being shoulder to shoulder produces an association that wouldn't be there otherwise.*

Yes, that's right. I can see dimly how all these things interconnect. One of the other things which I think are interesting is the constantly turning faces of that particular cube which on one side says for example: 'All Italians are voluble' and on the next side says, 'That is a naïve generalization'; and then, 'No it's not. Behind generalizations there must be some sort of basis'. Tilt it once more and there's the 'Yes, but . . .'. Then you're back to the original one. Do you see what I mean? I begin to think that the sophisticated perception is that the naïve generalization is a useful 'truth'. I'm fascinated by the correspondence between easy stereotypes and truth. Because there is one.

If you think about it, *Dirty Linen* is a play in which a sexy dumb blonde walks on and is utterly patronized, and the play ends with the entire committee adopting the resolution which she said they ought to adopt on page four or whatever it is. She actually is Miss Common Sense rather than Miss Empty Head. Probably she wasn't properly established before she begins to show other sides to herself, but certainly the idea is that she's anybody's plaything, totally empty-headed, with a big bust, and occasionally makes comments which are disquietingly irrefutable, and ends up by controlling the whole committee. If one did the play again it would probably take three acts and be a Major Work, but to hell with that.

It is this thing of stereotypes. I hate 'em and love 'em. I hate the cheapness of cheap television portrayal, where Frenchmen are like Maurice Chevalier and journalists wear trilby hats and drink a lot, but what's fascinating to me is that many Frenchmen *are* like Maurice Chevalier, and not many journalists go around with rimless glasses saying, 'No thank you, I'll have an orange juice'.

How did you react to Clive James's article about you in the November 1975 Encounter?

Clive is a very good example of this person who does a bit of everything and keeps thinking he doesn't do anything well enough. He's a very gifted man who reviews television, writes poetry, writes essays, I believe has written a play and is a joker, and a general sort of wag about town. I adore people like that. His piece in *Encounter* got it right, and he hadn't even seen the plays. He'd seen one and read the others. What he said was that you get into trouble with my plays if you think that there's a static viewpoint on the events. There is no observer. There is no safe point around which everything takes its proper place, so that you see things flat and see how they relate to each other. Although the Einsteinian versus Copernican image sounds pretentious, I can't think of a better one to explain what he meant—that there's no point of rest. I thought it was a brilliant piece, and what I like about Clive is that he reads the plays and sits down at ten o'clock in the morning and types. And the day after tomorrow, he's done that, and he'll go and do a piece on William Empson or dogs fouling the pavements.

Is economy a conscious issue with you?

Using things again and again, you mean?

Not wasting space. Going back to the goldfish in Jumpers. *Working for a maximum richness of texture.*

Economy isn't the word I'd use for that, though I know what you mean. It's not for economy's sake. It's just to fold things back on themselves so that they get thicker. Actually economy is a good word, but it's not because I'm being economical. The effect of elegant economy is something we all respond to. If you can use the same thing in three different ways it's artistically satisfactory. But then these things build themselves, you know. For example, when the Chairman in *Dirty Linen* tears up the five pound note, it's not as good as George stepping on the tortoise, but it's that sort of moment for the audience. Needless to say, *Dirty Linen* was written without that moment, because *New-Found-Land* hadn't been written. There wasn't any five pound note. So what is one actually doing? One is trying not to miss opportunities. That's what it's about, I think.

Maybe the fact of getting New-Found-Land *into* Dirty Linen *is relevant. You're terribly good at seams. You're very neat in your tailoring. There are never any rough edges or awkward corners or bulges.*

I really hate gratuitousness. On television—and I have enough technical knowledge about how plots work—if I see something which is a cheat on the one hand or a left-over on the other, or a little loose end, it destroys the entire edifice, as far as I'm concerned. To me it's like a bridge which is going to fall down in five minutes. I don't have a policy about this. It's not a principle. It's my temperament which forces it. Much writing about writers doesn't take this into account. Things are judged as if they were the writer's principles, and I'm convinced they're due to his temperament.

I think you do something to produce a climate in which the right kind of accidents tend to happen. Perhaps temperament induces habits and habits produce a system.

I find them quite extraordinary. They're just remarkable long shots—like James Joyce's middle name.[1] They're not even relevant to the way the play works. They're just like secrets which I have about the play, almost like little signs from God that you're on the right track.

[1] See page 3.